Science Magic
with Chemistry and Biology

Written by Ted Johnston, B.Sc., M.Ed., M.Phil., M.Inst.P., F.R.I.C.

Illustrated by Ben Manchip

PURNELL

Contents

For Alan

First published 1974 by Purnell Books
Berkshire House, Queen Street, Maidenhead, Berks.
Designed and produced for Purnell Books by
Intercontinental Book Productions
© 1974 Intercontinental Book Productions
Printed in Belgium by Henri Proost & Cie pvba

SBN 361 02992 6

BRANDESTON HALL
FRAMLINGHAM COLLEGE JUNIOR SCHOOL

THE   FORM 4B   PRIZE

for   PERSEVERANCE

Awarded to

M. P. JONES

19.6. 19 76   HEADMASTER

Provided the instructions given in this book are carefully followed all the experiments are quite harmless, and will provide a new and exciting way of discovering the "magic" of science.

Parents or teachers may wish to supervise the few experiments which require the use of heat, fire, electricity and gas.

Oak Apples

YOU WILL NEED:
oak apples
a knife
a magnifying glass
2 bowls
steel wool pad
vinegar
peroxide
a saucepan and the use of a cooker ring
a cup
drinking straws
scissors

Do you know the secret of the oak apples? Use your knife to cut through an oak apple. The magnifying glass will help you to unravel the mystery. Inside is curled a tiny grub. It lives inside until it is ready to eat its way out.

Oak apples and marble galls (the harder, rounder "apple") are caused by gall wasps. The female gall wasp lays her eggs in the fresh bud of an oak tree. This stops the bud forming into a leaf. Instead, an oak apple grows. You can use oak apples to make your own ink. Chop an oak apple into small pieces. Now soak these pieces in a bowl of water. **Figure 1.**

A substance called *tannin* is being extracted from the oak apples by the water. While the oak apple pieces are soaking, make some *iron acetate*. The iron you need is in the steel wool pad. If your pad has soap in it, this must be completely washed out. Put the clean steel wool pad into a saucepan and cover it with vinegar. **Figure 2.**

Boil for about five minutes. Allow to cool and to settle. You should, with care, be able to pour a little of the clear solution into a cup. **Figure 3.**

If you know how, it is better to filter the rather messy contents to get a clear solution in the cup. Add a few drops of peroxide to this solution. Do you see a change in the colour? You have made iron acetate solution. The iron in the steel wool joins with the acetic acid in the vinegar and with the hydrogen peroxide to form iron (ferric) acetate.

Now come back to your soaking oak apple pieces. Pour off as much liquid as possible into a bowl and add a few drops of the iron solution you have just made. Do you get a blue/black solution? You have made your own ink. **Figure 4.**

The iron acetate with the tannin from the oak apple produces iron tannate. It is this which gives the ink its colour. You could make the same ink by adding tea to the iron acetate.

Would you like a pen to use with your ink? You can make your own by cutting across a drinking straw, as shown in the large picture above. Your pen will write better if the slanting tip is dipped into a little detergent before use.

Colour a

YOU WILL NEED:
a white carnation
a dandelion root with leaves
2 jam jars
a pencil
red ink
black ink
a knife
an elastic band, or cotton

Plants need water. You have probably helped your parents to water plants. If you have indoor plants, you may simply have added water to the containers in which the plant pots stand. Does water travel upwards through to the top of the plant? See if you can find out, using these experiments.

Half-fill each of the jars with water. To one add red ink to colour the water red, and to the other add black ink to make black water. **Figure 1.**

Slit the stem of the carnation from the bottom for about 10 cm. Arrange the split stem so that one side is in the black solution and the other in the red solution. Support the carnation by fixing a pencil to the stem using an elastic band or some cotton thread. **Figure 2.**

Leave the carnation standing for several hours. Later you will find that one half of the flower is red and the other is black. What has happened?

All flowering plants have stems. Inside the stems are vessels, or tubes, through which water taken up by the roots travels upwards. The coloured water in this experiment lets you see the movement of water.

Top up the jar containing red-coloured water, so that it is half-full. Wash the dandelion root. **Figure 3.**

Put it into the red ink solution. Leave the root standing in the jar overnight. Remove the root and wash away the red ink. Using your knife, cut off the end of the root. What do you see? Carefully slice through the root. **Figure 4.**

The red ink has stained the tubes (vessels) which carry water through the root. Water travels through roots and through stems by way of water vessels in the roots and in the stems. It can move upwards through a plant. You can find out something more about the way water moves upwards by reading pages 10 and 11.

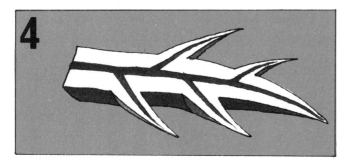

Patterns

YOU WILL NEED:
plain white paper
thick coloured crayons
selection of leaves

Would you like to start your own scrapbook of patterns from plants? Let's begin by taking rubbings of the barks of trees. Hold a sheet of white paper firmly against the bark of a tree and then rub a piece of thick crayon over the paper. **Figure 1.**

Keep the paper still while you are rubbing. You will soon see the bark pattern appear. **Figure 2.**

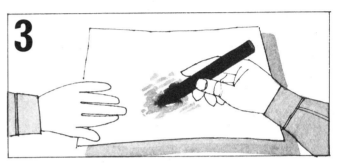

Use different-coloured crayons to find the best pattern. See what patterns you get from other trees. If you know the name of a tree, write it on the bark rubbing. Use the bark rubbing to give yourself ideas for painting or crayoning your own patterns on fresh paper. Put these into your scrapbook too. See if you can use your patterns to make a maze game for your friends . . . amaze them! Ask them if they can get from A to B without crossing a ridge.

Trees have a covering of bark over their trunks, stems, branches and roots to protect them. The bark keeps the tree watertight, but allows it to breathe. It is usually possible to tell one tree from another by comparing their barks. The bark of an oak tree is in ridges; the bark of the beech and of the silver birch is smooth. Your collection of rubbings will help you to identify trees.

You can take rubbings of leaves using the same method. Place a leaf on a flat table top and cover it with a piece of plain white paper. Hold the paper firmly with one hand, and with the other rub a piece of thick crayon over the surface of the paper covering the leaf. **Figure 3.**

Keep the paper still and you will see the leaf rubbing begin to appear. **Figure 4.**

Try different colours, as before, to find the best colour. Use different leaves. See if you can label your rubbings. Add all these to your scrapbook of patterns.

A network of lines can be seen on a leaf. These lines are very narrow tubes, called veins. They run down the stalk that joins the leaf to the stem, so that the leaf is connected to the root. Water can pass from the root to the leaves. There are many different kinds of leaf.

Capillarity

YOU WILL NEED:
3 strips of blotting paper, about 15 cm. long and
  4 cm. wide
4 strips of blotting paper, about 45 cm. long and
  4 cm. wide
3 glasses
blue ink
red ink
water
felt-tipped pens
a dish

Do you think that water can climb? It can. Here's how to watch it move upwards through blotting paper. You can make an interesting race too. Put about 3 cm. of water into each glass. Add a few drops of blue ink to one glass, making a blue solution, and a few drops of red ink to a second glass, making a red solution. Leave clear water in the third glass. Now put the end of each length of blotting paper into each glass. **Figure 1.**

Watch the blue water, the red water and the clear water race up the paper strips. Will they all reach the top of the paper? How long do they take to reach the top? Liquids, like the clear water and the coloured water in this experiment, can move up

through tiny openings. There are very many tiny openings in blotting paper, so that liquids can move up through them. Scientists say that liquids move in this way by *capillarity*. A capillary is a very narrow (hair-like) tube. It is important for plants that water can climb up the stems of the plant, so that water travels through the plant from the soil. There are narrow tubes in a plant stem. *Capillarity* helps the water to move up through the plant. You can make use of the fact that water goes up blotting paper strips.

Using a 45-cm. length of strip, make a small blot of black ink from a felt-tipped pen near the bottom of the paper, about 3 cm. from the end. Suspend the strip so that it can just dip into a dish of water placed beneath it. The end of the paper with the blot goes into the water, but the water must not touch or cover the blot. **Figure 2.**

The water will move up the paper, and the front of water soon reaches the ink spot. Now watch what happens. Can you see bright colours? What has happened to the black ink? Take the paper out and let it dry before the water front reaches the top of the strip.

You can invent another race game. Do the experiment again, using two strips with a different-coloured blot on each strip. Blue ink and black ink give good results. If your friend makes two strips as well, you can race the same colours against each other. If you have a large bowl of water, you

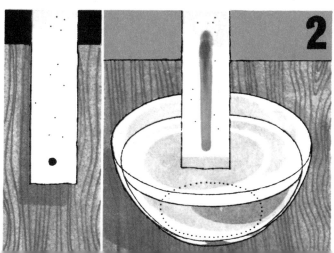

can use the same bowl for all the strips. It may save arguments about the winner.

Inks travel from a blot on a piece of blotting paper more slowly than the water in which they are dissolved. Some substances when dissolved in water travel more slowly than others up the paper. In this way a mixture of materials can be separated, the faster-moving substances quickly leaving the slower ones behind. Some inks are made up of a mixture of different colours and these will move at different speeds. You can see from your dried blotting paper, for example, that using black ink, the green and yellow colours move faster than the navy blue. You have separated the colours (pigments) that make up the black ink from a felt pen.

Making Chromatograms

YOU WILL NEED:
blotting paper
felt-tipped pens
an eye dropper or a straw
a saucer
a cup of water
scissors

Here is another colourful way of separating the colours in some inks. Cut a piece of blotting paper about 10 cm. square. Make a blob of ink in the middle from one of the felt-tipped pens. Place the blotting paper over the saucer.

Dip the eye dropper or the straw into the cup of water.

If you use an eye dropper, squeeze the bulb to get some water into the tube. If you use a straw, put your finger over the top to trap some water in the straw.

Carefully let one drop of water drip on to the ink blot. Wait a few seconds until the water stops spreading and add another drop. Keep doing this, but try to let the drops always fall in the same place, as near the middle of the blot as you can. Always wait until the water stops spreading before adding another drop.

As the water spreads out, it takes the ink with it. You now know that coloured materials spread at different speeds, so that they become separated out. The faster ones travel further and the slower

ones get left behind. As the pictures show, not all inks are mixtures. There has been no separation with the red one, for example, showing that there is just one colour in that particular red ink.

Try the experiment with other materials, such as ink from a bottle, or any colouring that your mother may use in the kitchen. Of course, the materials you use must dissolve in water or the experiment will not work.

Separating out things in the way shown on these pages is called *chromatography* and the patterns you have made are known as *chromatograms*. The word *"chromatography"* means colour writing.

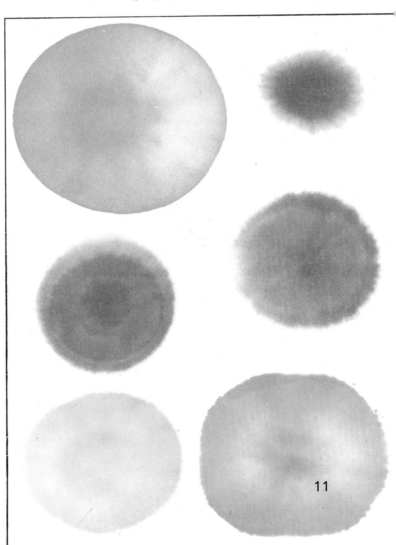

Making a Spirit Burner

YOU WILL NEED:
a small tin (such as a tobacco tin)
a piece of wood
a hammer and screwdriver
cotton wool
methylated spirit
a pair of pliers
a wire coathanger
a tin can

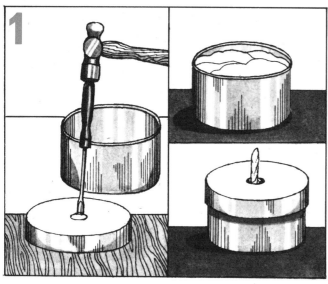

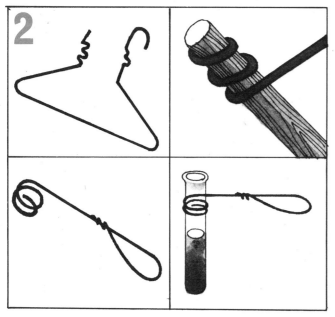

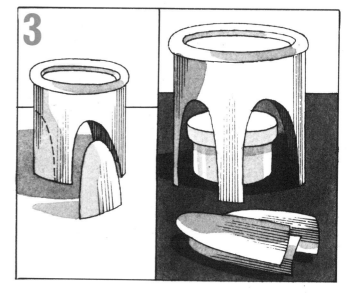

You can carry out many more interesting and exciting science experiments if you have a burner on which to heat things. Perhaps your mother will let you use a ring on the kitchen cooker when you need it. You will also need an old saucepan for experiments like the one on page 7. For some experiments, the heat from a candle flame will be sufficient. Or you can buy a simple glass spirit burner quite cheaply. Better still, you can make your own spirit burner for next to no cost.

Take the lid off your small tin. Place it on a piece of wood, and, using a hammer and screwdriver, knock a small hole about as big as a $\frac{1}{2}$-p coin in the middle. Pack the tin full of cotton wool. As you replace the lid, thread a tuft of cotton wool through the hole you have made, to serve as a wick. **Figure 1.**

To use the burner, pour in methylated spirit until the cotton wool is well soaked. Replace the lid and light the cotton tuft wick. Make sure you don't overfill the tin with spirit, and always keep the tin full of cotton wool. Stand the burner on a plate for safety.

The fuel for your spirit burner is alcohol. Alcohol passes up through the tuft wick by *capillarity*. It is the alcohol vapour which burns. Alcohol is highly inflammable.

Here are some more ideas for do-it-yourself apparatus. You can make your own test-tube holder from a wire coathanger. Use a pair of pliers to shape a test-tube holder like the one shown. **Figure 2.**

How about a tripod stand? You can make one from a tin can. Ask your father to help you cut away the sides from the can, and arrange your tripod to fit neatly over the burner, or see if you can make a tripod from a wire coathanger. **Figure 3.**

A Camphor Boat

YOU WILL NEED:
camphor
milk bottle tops (aluminium)
used matchsticks
glue
scissors
a large bowl
coloured paper

Clean a metal milk bottle top very thoroughly so that it is free from grease. Smooth out the foil and use your scissors to shape it into the outline of a boat, about 3 cm. long. **Figure 4.**

Cut a V-shape notch in the stern and then fix a small piece of camphor in it. **Figure 5.**

Glue a used matchstick to the boat to serve as a mast. You can use coloured paper to make a sail. **Figure 6.**

Now that your boat is ready, you must find a "lake" for it to sail on. Carefully clean out the large bowl, using hot water and detergent. The bowl must be free from grease. Rinse out the bowl well and half-fill it with water. Your boat, placed on the surface, will now move magically across the "lake". **Figure 7.**

If the boat stops, rinse out the bowl and change the water. Why not make two boats and have a race?

The boat is able to work because there is a pull in the surface of water, called *surface tension*. The camphor jammed at the stern of the boat slowly dissolves. This makes *camphor solution*—camphor dissolved in water—near the back of your boat. The surface tension of camphor solution is less than that of plain water. The pull of the plain water in front of the boat is greater than the pull of the camphor solution behind. The boat moves forward.

Similar boats may be driven by a little detergent powder, or by drops of methylated spirit.

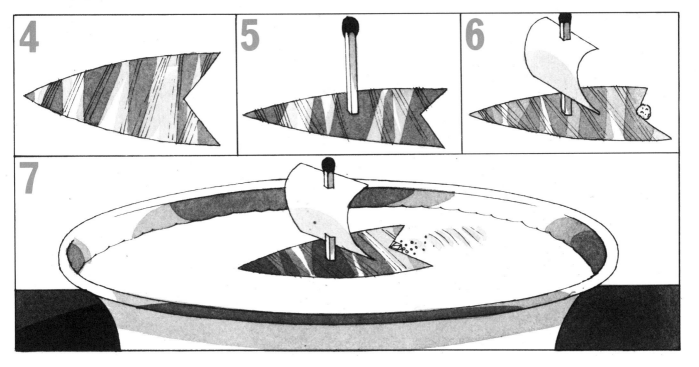

Wonderful Crystals

YOU WILL NEED:
a pie dish and a jam jar
hot water·salt
a magnifying glass or a projector
clear adhesive tape
a flannel
blotting paper

Grains of salt are very interesting to look at, but the trouble is that they are too small to be seen clearly with the naked eye. If you have a magnifying glass or a microscope you will be able to see the detail more clearly.

Perhaps there is a projector in the house which you could use. Set it up and find an old colour slide that is no longer needed. Take out the celluloid picture, leaving just the frame of cardboard or plastic. Stick a piece of clear tape across the hole and sprinkle salt grains on to the sticky side of the tape. Put the slide in the projector and switch on. When magnified, the shape of the salt crystals may be seen more clearly. They are tiny cubes, often very regular in their appearance. **Figure 1.**

Although a lot of salt together looks white, the indi-vidual crystals are colourless. This is because they allow most of the light to pass through them. But when there are millions of crystals all together in a dish they reflect the light and appear white.

Another way to see the detailed shape of crystals is to make them grow bigger. To do this, put some hot water in the jam jar and add as much salt as will dissolve, stirring all the time. It does not matter if you add too much salt. **Figure 2**

Carefully pour the liquid into the pie dish, leaving behind in the jar any of the undissolved salt.

Put the pie dish away in a place where it will not be disturbed, covering it with the flannel. If you can find a warm spot, near a radiator or in the airing cupboard, so much the better. Look at the dish from time to time, but, although you can remove the flannel, try not to disturb the dish itself. Leave it until the salt crystals have grown to a good size. **Figure 3**.

Choose a large salt crystal. Dry it on blotting paper and then examine it under a magnifying glass. Draw the shape of your salt crystal.

The salt in the packet or in the salt-cellar consists of very tiny crystals. Salt is purified by dissolving it in water and then letting it crystallise out. But the salt maker does not have your patience, and makes

the crystals form very quickly so that they do not have time to grow very much. Letting them form more slowly, in the pie dish, enables larger crystals to form. You can try the same experiments with different kinds of sugar.

Stringing Along

YOU WILL NEED:
sugar
Epsom salt
a pencil
cotton thread
3 tumblers
a cup and saucer
a teaspoon
a paper clip

Pour some boiling water into a cup and add sugar while stirring. Keep adding sugar until no more will dissolve. Do this as quickly as possible so that the solution stays hot. Now pour the hot sugar solution into one of the tumblers. **Figure 1.**

Hang a thread into the solution, using your pencil as support. A paper clip tied to the end of the thread will help to weigh the thread down. **Figure 2.**

Put the tumbler away in a warm place. Leave it for a day. When you come back you will find the thread covered with beautiful sugar crystals. Hot water usually dissolves more of a solid substance than the same amount of cold water. The cool solution can no longer keep all the sugar dissolved in it. This sugar comes out of solution as lovely crystals. Examine them under your magnifying glass. Try drawing one.

Dissolve the Epsom salt in hot water in one of the tumblers. Keep adding the salt until no more will dissolve. Do the same for a second tumbler. Now join the tumblers by a cotton thread—each end dipping well beneath the surface of the liquids in the tumblers. Place a saucer beneath the lowest part of your hanging thread. **Figure 3.**

Leave your experiment in a safe place. Come back after a day. You will find wonderful shapes hanging from the thread. Other crystals will be formed on the saucer. These came from drips from the thread.

Figure 4.

The Epsom salt solution moved along the thread by capillarity. When the solution cooled, *crystals* of Epsom salt formed.

Taking Apart and Putting Together

YOU WILL NEED:
iron filings
salt
a magnet
a piece of white paper
a magnifying glass
a cup

Take a teaspoonful of iron filings and a teaspoonful of salt. Mix them well together on the piece of

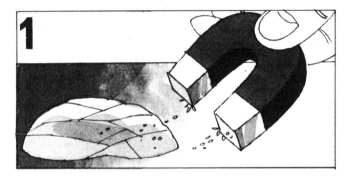

paper. Look closely at this mixture through your magnifying glass. Can you still see the salt clearly? Can you see the iron filings? How can you separate the iron from the salt? An easy way is to use your magnet. The magnet picks the iron out of the mixture. The salt is left behind. **Figure 1.**

Magnets attract to themselves magnetic substances like iron and steel. They do not attract non-magnetic substances like salt, sugar and sulphur. The iron and the salt have not been changed by mixing them together on the paper. Have you any other ideas for separating iron and salt? Salt dissolves very easily in water. Iron does not dissolve. This will give you a clue.

Make another mixture of iron and salt. Put it into your cup. Half-fill the cup with water and stir the mixture. Soon you will be able to see only iron filings in the cup. The salt has dissolved. You could *filter* this mixture.

Make a Filter

YOU WILL NEED:
a paper towel
scissors
a saucer
an empty yoghurt carton (flat bottomed type)
a glass jar
a hammer and a small nail
a pencil

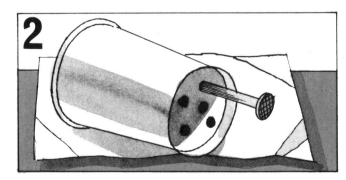

Stand your yoghurt carton on a paper towel. Draw a circle round the bottom of the carton with your pencil. Now cut out the circle of paper. This is your filter paper. Use a nail to punch four or five holes in the bottom of the carton. **Figure 2.**

Push the filter paper into the carton to fit inside the bottom, over the holes. Put the carton on top of the jar. Now stir up your mixture in the cup. Then pour it very slowly into the carton. **Figure 3.**

What is left on the filter paper? What goes through it into the jar? The liquid, which is a solution of salt dissolved in water, is able to pass through the tiny holes in the paper towel. The solid iron filings are not. The solid left behind on a filter paper is called the *residue.* The clear liquid passing through is called the *filtrate.*

Pour the filtrate from your experiment into a saucer. Leave it for several days. On your return you will find only solid salt in the saucer. The liquid has gone. Here you have separated salt and water. The water *evaporates* (changes into water vapour) from the salt solution. Tiny particles of water, called *molecules*, slowly escape from the solution. They go into the air as water vapour. The salt is left behind in the saucer.

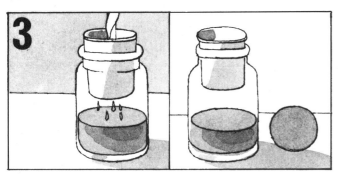

Iron and Sulphur Magic

YOU WILL NEED:
iron filings
sulphur (flowers of sulphur)
a magnet
a magnifying glass
a cup and saucer
an old teaspoon

Make a mixture of iron filings and sulphur in the same way that you made a mixture of iron and salt,

only this time take more trouble with the amounts you use. Take one teaspoonful of iron and two teaspoonsful of sulphur. **Figure 4.**

Have a look at this new mixture through your magnifying glass. Can you still see the iron and sulphur clearly? How will you separate them? Use the magnet again. **Figure 5.**

Collect the iron filings from the magnet and make the iron/sulphur mixture again. Put your mixture into the cup, and stand this in its saucer. Try this experiment: add a little water to the cup—just enough to make a paste when you stir. **Figure 6.**

You will feel the cup get hot. Take care—it can get as hot as a boiling kettle. Watch and listen. Steam is given off. Do you smell sulphur? After about 20 minutes the cup should have cooled. When it is cool, have a close look at its contents. Does it look different from iron and sulphur? It should.

You have made a new chemical called *iron sulphide*. It is a fine black powder. You will not be able to separate iron and sulphur from this, either by hand or with your magnet. **Figure 7.**

Your iron and sulphur have *combined* together chemically to form a chemical *compound* called iron sulphide. When chemical reactions like this take place, heat is usually given off. You saw the heat of the reaction taking place in the cup.

Chemical *compounds* are quite different from *mixtures*. Compounds are often quite different from the chemicals from which they are made. You cannot get back by simple methods the substances with which you started.

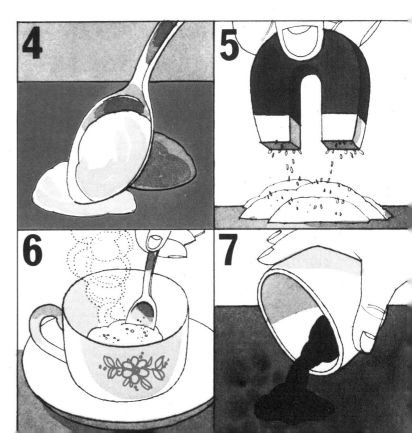

Plants and Oxygen

YOU WILL NEED:
a test-tube
a glass funnel
a large glass, or clear plastic jar
water weed
a wooden splint

If you get a chance, have a close look at an aquarium which is standing in sunlight. There will probably be green plants growing in it. Some of these plants will have tiny bubbles of gas collecting on them and rising to the surface of the water. Let's see if you can find out what is happening.

Place the water weed on the bottom of your jar and stand the glass funnel to cover *most* of the weed. **Figure 1.**

It's best to keep a gap between the bottom of the jar and the funnel—the trapped pieces of weed will do this for you. Pour water into the jar until it is almost full. Hold the test-tube under the water in the jar so that the tube fills completely with water. You must get rid of all the air that was in the tube. Now place your filled test-tube over the stem of the funnel.

Stand your jar in strong sunlight. Return to examine your experiment in about an hour. Do you see bubbles of gas rising out of the plant? **Figure 2.**

These bubbles will rise up the stem of the funnel and displace water in the test-tube. Leave the experiment again for several hours—until the test-tube is full of gas. Take the test-tube out of the water, keeping your thumb tightly over the end. Try to keep the test-tube upside-down. This will help to prevent any gas escaping. Now light a thin splint of wood. Blow out the flame and push the still-glowing splint into the test-tube. The splint will start to burn again. The gas in the test-tube has relit a glowing splint. The gas is *oxygen*. (Scientists use this method as a test for oxygen.) **Figure 3**.

Try the experiment again—this time standing your jar in a dark place. You will find that no gas will come off the green plant. It works only in strong light.

You know that you use oxygen when you breathe.

Many living things use up oxygen. Why is it not soon all used up?

Although oxygen is being taken from the air, green plants are putting oxygen back into the air. They do it only when light is shining on them. This light comes from the sun. In this way green plants take in carbon dioxide and turn it into oxygen. **Figure 4.**

A healthy aquarium has plants growing in it to supply the water with oxygen for the fish. Some aquariums have air bubbled through the water as well. Then the fish have plenty of oxygen.

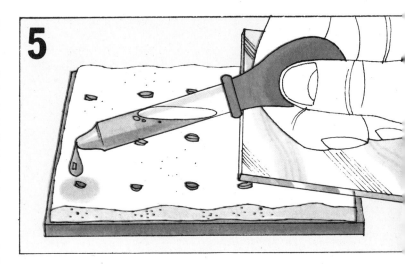

Learning about Roots

YOU WILL NEED:
a piece of hardboard or very thick card
a piece of glass about the same size
a large piece of cotton wool
seeds—mustard and cress
2 large rubber bands
a medicine dropper and some water

How clever is a root? You may be surprised. See what you think when you have done this.

Place the hardboard or card flat on a table and cover it with a layer of cotton wool. Arrange a few seeds on the cotton wool. Use the medicine dropper to make the cotton wool damp all over, but do not soak it too much. Place the glass over the top.

Strap the whole lot together with the rubber bands and stand the experiment upright on a windowsill, preferably in a warm, sunny position. Use the medicine dropper to keep the seeds moist.

After a day or two, the seeds should begin to grow. When the roots are about 2 cm. long, rotate the apparatus by a quarter turn. After some more growth, give another turn. What do you notice? The stems and roots will have changed their direction of growth. Why do you think this is?

Roots grow downwards because that is where they would normally find water in the soil. Leaves and stems grow upwards towards the light. The downward growth of the roots is called *geotropism*, and the upward growth of the stems and leaves is called *heliotropism*.

move to the edge of the jar. Now drop some small pieces of candle wax on to the surface. These will also collect together, but they will move to the middle of the jar!

Using your jug, carefully fill the jar right to the top with more water until the liquid is almost overflowing. Notice the bulging water surface. What happens to the wood and wax? They change

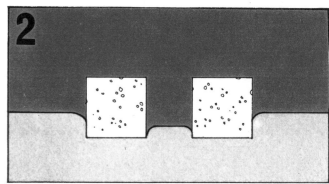

places! The wood moves to the middle, and the wax to the side. More science magic!

Wood is "wet" by water, which means that water clings to it. The water, in fact, climbs a little way up the side of the wood, and if two pieces of wood are close together, the water levels look like those in **Figure 1**.

Because of these different levels, there is a pressure from the outside forcing the pieces of wood together. Wax is *not* wet by water, and when

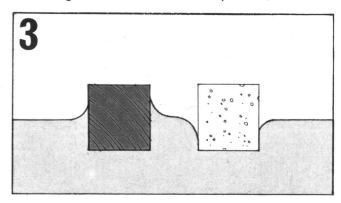

two pieces of wax are close together, the water levels look like those in **Figure 2**.

Again there is an outside pressure forcing the wax together. Wood and wax will stay apart because their water levels are like those in **Figure 3**.

Play the wax-match game. Why not race your pieces of wood? Clean out the jar. Fill it almost to the top with water. Drop your pieces of wood into the centre and let them race to the side. It's more fun if your friend races his wood against yours.

Wood and Water

YOU WILL NEED:
a narrow jar
used matchsticks (or wooden splints)
a candle end
a small jug

Have you noticed that pieces of wood floating on a pond tend to gather together? What do you think causes this? Let's see if this experiment will give you some ideas. Wash out the glass jar with detergent so that it is free from grease. Rinse the jar well. Fill it almost to the top with water. Now take some small pieces of clean wooden splints or used matchsticks. If you use matchsticks, it's best to soak them in boiling water first.

Drop three or four small pieces of wood one by one on to the middle of the water surface. Watch closely. The sticks will group together and then

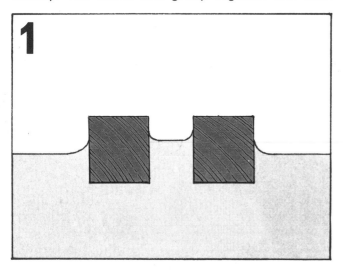

Wax and Water

YOU WILL NEED:
a spirit burner as on page 12
candle wax
a tin lid
2 wire (or zinc) gauze squares
a large dish or bowl
an old kitchen sieve

Slightly turn up the edges of the gauze. Dip it, in sections at a time, in melted wax. You can melt the candle wax in the tin lid using your spirit burner. Shake the gauze over some paper, so that each strand of wire has a coating of wax yet the holes stay clear. Make sure the bowl is clean and half-fill it with water. Place the waxed gauze in the water.

It will float! Try putting a light toy on it. **Figure 1.**

Now try to float an unwaxed gauze and watch it sink. In the same way, wax the gauze of the kitchen sieve. Again keep the holes clear. Add water to the sieve. Yes, the holes will hold water! **Figure 2.**

Waxing the wire makes it a material which is not wet by water. The surface tension of the water pushes upwards, supporting the gauze. A similar push keeps the water in the sieve.

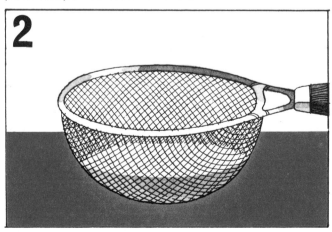

Fire and Water

YOU WILL NEED:
a narrow bandage
methylated spirit (or surgical spirit)
a glass jar
2 test-tube holders as on page 12

Do this experiment over a sink. You will need two test-tube holders. The home-made ones will do fine.

Fill the jar almost to the top with a mixture of half water and half methylated (or surgical) spirit. Cut two lengths of bandage, each about 20 cm. long.

Dip one of these into the meths./water mixture, so that the bandage is well soaked. Leave the other bandage strip quite dry. Hold the two strips by the test-tube holders over the sink at arm's length. Ask your friend to set fire to each piece with a match. Watch carefully. The dry bandage burns, but the soaked strip is not damaged by the flames around it.

The methylated spirit (which is mostly ethyl alcohol—or ethanol) burns, but is used up before any of the bandage is burned. The water left in the bandage stops it from catching fire.

Invisible Inks

YOU WILL NEED:
a lemon
an old-fashioned nib pen or mapping pen (a
**   sharpened matchstick or toothpick will do)**
a candle
white paper
3 egg-cups
an onion
an old teaspoon
alum
milk

Lemon Ink

Cut a lemon in half. Squeeze out the juice into an egg cup. This is your ink-well! Make sure the nib of your pen is clean then write your secret message, using the lemon juice as ink. **Figure 1.**

Allow the writing to dry and it becomes invisible! If you want a friend to read it, warm the paper carefully over the lighted candle. Hold it about 6–8 cm. above the flame. Keep moving the paper so that no one spot is heated too strongly. Soon your message will appear in light brown ink. **Figure 2.**

A substance has to be heated to its *ignition temperature* before it will burn. The lemon juice contains citric acid. When the juice dries, citric acid is left on the paper. Citric acid and paper have *different* ignition temperatures. Citric acid burns (*oxidises*) before the paper is affected. The heat made the citric acid ink join with the oxygen in the air. The citric acid was *oxidised*.

Onion Ink

Now let's see how well the onion juice works. Stick your pen into a piece of onion and use it just as you used the lemon juice. You will find that onion juice is a good secret ink too!

Milk Ink

Pour some milk into the second egg cup. Use the milk as ink in the same way that you used lemon juice and onion juice. When the milk is dry, your writing is invisible. If you warm the invisible writing over a candle flame, the words will be seen written in a brown ink.

The onion juice and the milk work in the same way as the lemon juice. They are burnt (oxidised) to a brown colour before the paper is affected.

Secret Messages

YOU WILL NEED:
phenolphthalein solution
ammonia solution (dilute)
a nib pen and holder
white paper

If you have no phenolphthalein, you can make your own. The instructions are on page 59. To make the best ink, have a solution of phenolphthalein in equal parts of surgical spirit and water. So you will need to add water to a solution of phenolphthalein in spirit. **Figure 3.**

Now write a secret message on the paper. When the writing is dry, it is completely invisible. To bring the words back, moisten the writing with ammonia solution. **Figure 4.**

What do you see? A bright red message! But it disappears when the page becomes dry. Real magic here to baffle your friends! And you can always bring the writing back again by dabbing with more ammonia. If you want the writing to stay longer, use washing soda to dab the ink instead of ammonia. This will be visible for days.

Black Mark Black Spot
Would you like to make a black mark to give to your friends? It will be like the famous black spot of *Treasure Island*, but your black spot will be secret. It will be invisible.

Mix half a teaspoonful of alum with some water in an egg cup. Use this solution as your ink. You can make a big spot on a piece of paper. Let your magic ink dry. When it is dry, you will find that it is invisible. To bring it back into sight, you need to warm the paper over the candle flame. This time your ink will be *black*: a black spot. You can use your alum ink, of course, for ordinary writing too. It will always come out black.

The alum ink burns (oxidises) before the paper is affected by the heat from the candle. This time your burnt (oxidised) ink is black.

Phenolphthalein is an *indicator*. This means that it changes colour in the presence of an *acid* or *alkali*. Phenolphthalein is red in alkali solution and colourless in acid or neutral solution. Your phenolphthalein change to a red colour because ammonia solution is an alkali. Any alkali would produce the colour change. Washing soda or ordinary soapy water will do the trick. Ammonia evaporates quickly, and so has the most magical effect, because the writing so soon disappears again.

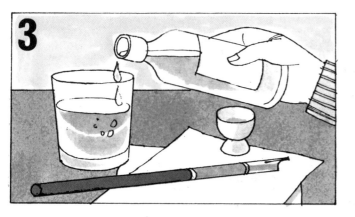

Magic in the Air

Push one of these moistened tufts into the bottom of the test-tube. Do not pack it too tightly. Keep the rest of the wool for other experiments. Stand the tube upside-down in about 3 cm. of water in the tumbler. **Figure 2.**

Place the tumbler and its contents in a safe place. Mark the level of water in the test-tube, using your wax pencil. The experiment takes about two days. Mark the level of the water in the test-tube about every 12 hours. **Figure 3.**

What do you notice? Does the level change? Does the steel wool change? Can you see rust forming on the steel tuft? Leave the tube set up until there is no further change in the level of water. The water will have risen about one-fifth of the way up the test-tube. Examine the rusted wool. Notice how different rust is from iron.

YOU WILL NEED:
a steel wool pad
vinegar
a jam jar with cover
a tumbler
a test-tube
a wax pencil

This is a famous experiment! Iron is allowed to rust in air. Your iron is in the steel wool pad. Steel is mostly iron. The pad probably has a coating of anti-rust on it, so for best results you must remove it. To do this, put the steel wool pad in your jam jar. Add enough strong vinegar solution to cover it. **Figure 1.**

Place the lid on the jar and leave the steel wool to soak overnight. You have pickled the steel! Next day, drain off the vinegar and well-rinse the steel pad in water. Break up the pad into about five fluffy tufts.

You can use the same test-tube to see if the amount of pickled steel makes any difference to the height the water rises. Does the position of the steel in the tube make any difference? Try jamming a tuft about half-way up the test-tube. You should find that each time the water rises about one-fifth up the test-tube. Your changes make no difference. The steel wool rusts inside the test-tube. As this happens, the water rises. This shows that some of the air around the steel wool is being removed. The water rises up the tube to take its place. This keeps the air pressures equal. (Why do you think the pressure inside the tube became less than that outside?)

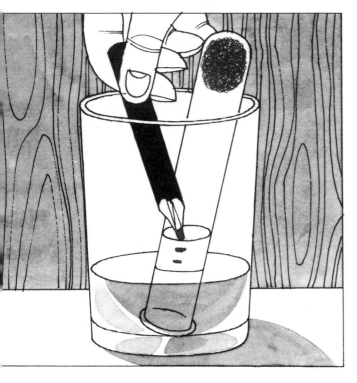

Air is a mixture of gases. One of these gases is oxygen. When steel rusts, the iron in the steel joins with oxygen from the air. It is the oxygen which is slowly all used up. The air is made up of about one-fifth oxygen. The rust formed is a compound of iron, oxygen and water.

Frothy Fun

YOU WILL NEED:
a tall jar
a bowl
hydrogen peroxide
manganese dioxide
wooden splints
liquid detergent

Stand the tall jar in the bowl. Pour some hydrogen peroxide into this jar to a depth of about 2 cm. Add about a half-teaspoonful of liquid detergent, and mix this with the hydrogen peroxide by swirling the jar. Add a *little* manganese dioxide to the mixture in the jar: Watch! What a froth! **Figure 4.**

Do the experiment again, *without* adding the liquid detergent. Light a wooden splint. Then blow it out. While it is still glowing, push it into the jar. It will relight. Oxygen is in the jar. This is your test for oxygen.

When manganese dioxide is added to hydrogen peroxide, oxygen gas is formed. There is a fizzing in the solution and you will see lots of bubbles. This is the oxygen gas coming off. Oxygen gas will relight a glowing splint. The liquid detergent you

added to the hydrogen peroxide is frothed up by the oxygen.

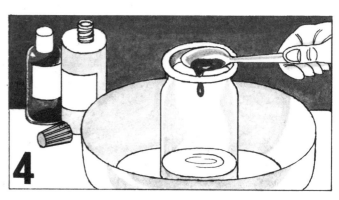

Oxygen Magic

YOU WILL NEED:
household bleach
blue/black writing ink
a tumbler
a jam jar
a spoon

Half-fill the jam jar with water. Add a few drops of blue/black writing ink and stir. Pour five or six drops of your bleach into the tumbler and half-fill this with water.

Carefully pour a little of this bleach solution into the jam jar. What happens? Real magic! The blue water becomes clear again! Now you can truly amaze your friends. **Figure 5.**

Common household bleaches owe their whitening action to oxygen. Their oxygen joins with the colouring matter with which they are in contact to give a new substance. This new substance is usually white. That's why bleaches are used to whiten laundry. In your experiment the colouring of the ink was removed by bleach.

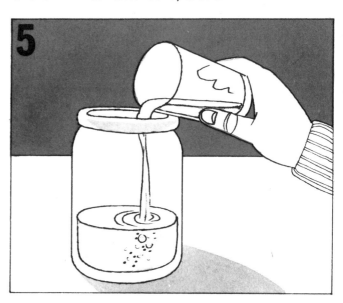

The Magic Power of Yeast

YOU WILL NEED:
hydrogen peroxide
yeast powder
2 tumblers
a test-tube
a wooden splint
a candle
string
a quart bottle
sugar
a balloon
limewater
an old spoon

Half-fill your tumbler with water. Take a pinch of yeast powder and drop it into the test-tube. Carefully add hydrogen peroxide to this yeast until the test-tube is full. Place your thumb quickly over the mouth of the test-tube. **Figure 1.**

Turn the tube upside-down, keeping your thumb firmly in place to prevent peroxide coming out. Place the tube upside-down under the water in the tumbler. Remove your thumb, so that the test-tube rests on the bottom of the tumbler. **Figure 2.**

Watch the test-tube. Bubbles of gas collect in the top of the tube. The liquid in the tube is pushed downwards. Soon the tube is full of gas. Now for some detective work! What gas is it?

Take the test-tube from the water, firmly covering its mouth with your thumb. Light the splint. Blow it out and then push the *glowing* splint into the test-tube. It relights and burns very brightly. Your gas is oxygen. **Figure 3.**

Hydrogen peroxide is a substance which is made up of hydrogen and oxygen joined together chemi-

cally. If the oxygen can be freed, then you have a way of making oxygen. In fact, hydrogen peroxide solution, such as the one you have, slowly changes into oxygen and water by itself anyway. The yeast helps the change to take place much more quickly.

The yeast is acting here as a *catalyst*. A catalyst changes the speed of a chemical reaction without itself being changed. The manganese dioxide in the experiment on page 25 acted in a similar way.

Yeast will help you to make another gas. Half-fill your second tumbler with warm water. Add about four teaspoonsful of sugar and stir with the spoon

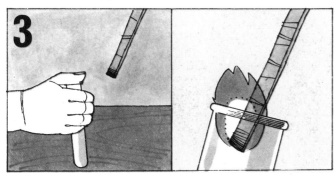

until the sugar has dissolved. Pour your sugar solution into the large bottle. It may help if you pour your sugar solution from a clean jug. Now wash out the tumbler. Use it to mix one teaspoonful of yeast in a little water. Add this mixture to the sugar solution in the bottle. **Figure 4.**

Blow up the balloon several times, so that the rubber becomes stretched. This will help it to blow up more easily during the experiment. Let out the air and fix the balloon to the neck of the bottle. Tie it on *tightly* with a piece of string.

Put your bottle, with the balloon attached, in a safe

and warm place. It will be at least half an hour before you see much happening. Can you see bubbles? What can you hear? What can you smell? Notice what begins to happen to the balloon. About every half hour give the bottle a gentle shake. Your balloon will eventually be blown up by gas made inside the bottle. **Figure 5.**

After two or three hours, untie (or cut) the string and remove the balloon from the bottle. Quickly twist the neck of the balloon to keep the gas trapped inside.

Half-fill a tumbler with limewater. Hold the neck of the balloon under the limewater. Now slowly release some of the gas from the balloon, so that it bubbles through the limewater. **Figure 6.**

You will find that the limewater turns milky. What was the gas in the balloon? Now watch the rest of the gas putting out a candle flame. Your gas is carbon dioxide.

Yeast is alive! It is made up of thousands of tiny

yeast plants that will grow and multiply, given the right conditions. The sugar is food for the yeast plants. To grow, these need food, air, water and the correct temperature. As they grow, the plants form important chemicals called *enzymes*. These break down the sugar into *alcohol* and *carbon dioxide*. Your own body needs enzymes. They help break down food in your stomach. The smell you noticed was alcohol. The bubbling you saw was caused by the carbon dioxide gas. You collected this gas in the balloon. Your tests showed that it was carbon dioxide.

Mothball Bouncers

YOU WILL NEED:
a tumbler
mothballs
baking soda
vinegar
an old tablespoon

Have some fun with mothballs. Try putting some into a glass of water. They sink but they will rise in water if you give them each a little "lifebelt". Fill the tumbler almost to the top with water. Add two tablespoonsful of vinegar and two tablespoonsful of baking soda. **Figure 1.**

Stir the contents of the tumbler until the baking soda has dissolved. Now add three of your mothballs. They still sink to the bottom. But if you put the tumbler in a safe place, and leave it for an hour or two, you will be surprised at the change taking place. The mothballs are "bouncing" up and down in the glass! Look carefully and you will see their lifebelts made of tiny bubbles! They cling to each mothball.

Your mothballs will keep dancing until all the chemicals are used up. This may take several days

—time enough to amaze your friends with more science magic. Mothballs are slightly denser than water, so usually they will sink. Baking soda and vinegar make carbon dioxide gas.

Bubbles of this gas can be seen in the tumbler—around the sides and on the bottom. Even more of them cling to the rough surface of the mothballs. They act like tiny lifebelts, raising a mothball to the surface. When they reach the surface, some bubbles break off. Then the mothballs sink until they collect enough bubbles to bring them to the top again.

Make a Snowstorm...

YOU WILL NEED:
boric acid
a tumbler
a bowl
a spirit burner and stand
a clean tin can
an old tablespoon

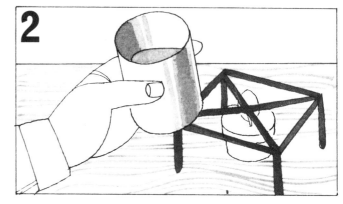

Half-fill à tumbler with water. Add three table-spoons of boric acid and stir. Pour the solution into the tin can and place this over the lighted spirit burner. **Figure 2.** Your home-made burner (page 12) will do fine.

Heat the solution until it is boiling. Take care! Stir until all the boric acid has dissolved. Stand your tumbler in a bowl of cold water. Add the hot solution from the can, taking care to protect your hands. **Figure 3.**

Now watch the solution cool. Do you see "snow-flakes" falling through it? You have made a magic snow scene. Most solid substances dissolve more easily in hot water than in cold water. This is true of boric acid too. The hot water can hold more of the acid dissolved in it than the cold water. As the solution cools, some boric acid does not remain dissolved. It appears as the white solid—which makes your snowflakes. Do you know what real snowflakes are made of? Why do they float so gently from the sky? What are they floating on?

...and a Snowman

YOU WILL NEED:
an 8-cm. length of pipe cleaner
a glass jar with a screwtop lid
mothball crystals
a clothes peg
plaster
an old saucer
an old teaspoon
cotton wool

First make your model snowman, using the clothes peg as his body. Cut an 8-cm. length of pipe cleaner. Twist it around the jaws of the peg to serve as his arms. Trap a ball of cotton wool in the tips of the jaws to make a white face. **Figure 4.**

Mix a stiff paste of plaster on the saucer and place a small mound of it in the lid of the jar. Push the "legs" of the snowman into the mound. **Figure 5.**

Leave it to dry in position on the lid. Make sure that the edges and inner thread of the lid are clear of plaster, or the lid will not screw back on the jar. Fill the jar with water and add half a teaspoonful of mothball crystals to it. The crystals will not dissolve.

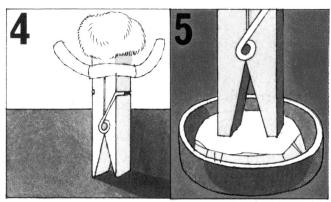

Carefully screw the lid back on the jar. Make sure the plaster mould is not damaged. Turn the jar to stand on its lid. The mothball snowflakes drop slowly over and around your snowman. **Figure 6.**

Mothball crystals (which are a chemical called *naphthalene*) do not dissolve in water. The crystals are only slightly more dense than water, so that they drift gently to the bottom of the jar.

You could soak the pipe cleaner arms of your snowman in cobalt chloride solution, as described overleaf. If you now paint your snowman's body white, you can make a snowman whose arms go from blue to pink when he first stands in the snowstorm in your jar. His body stays white.

29

Would you like to make a magic weather man who changes colour when it's going to rain? Take about two teaspoonsful of cobalt chloride and dissolve it, with stirring, in some water in your cup. It will make a pink solution. Cut a 6-cm. length of pipe cleaner and use this as the man's body. Take an 8-cm. length of cleaner and twist it around the body, about 3 cm. from the top, to form two arms of equal length. Attach another 8-cm. length of pipe cleaner to the end of the body to give two legs. **Figure 1**.

Now soak the man (he will bend easily) in the pink solution in the cup. **Figure 2**.

Take him out to dry. While he's drying, paint a man's face on a cork, using felt pens. Have a close look at the pipe cleaner part of your man when he's dried out. He's changed from pink to blue!

Spike the cork on the top of the body to complete your magic weather man. In damp weather he'll be pink. **Figure 3**. In dry weather he'll be blue. **Figure 4**.

You might like to make him hold a sign that says: "Pink I'm wet. Blue I'm dry." Your weather man should let you know when it's going to rain.

As you have seen, cobalt chloride changes colour from pink to blue when it becomes drier. But it is able to reverse this change and go from pink to blue if it is dampened again. The colour change works both ways! We can use cobalt chloride as a test for water. Scientists do this by means of paper which has been soaked in cobalt chloride and then dried. These cobalt chloride papers are used as test papers in laboratories, so that scientists are able to track down water.

Use magical cobalt chloride to make a colourful submarine. Soak your pipe cleaner in cobalt chloride as before, and allow it to dry. Then shape a submarine, which will have a pink part under

Weather Man

YOU WILL NEED:
cobalt chloride
pipe cleaners
a cork
a cup
felt-tipped pen

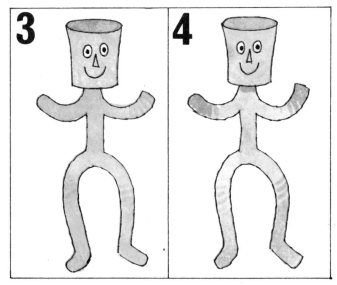

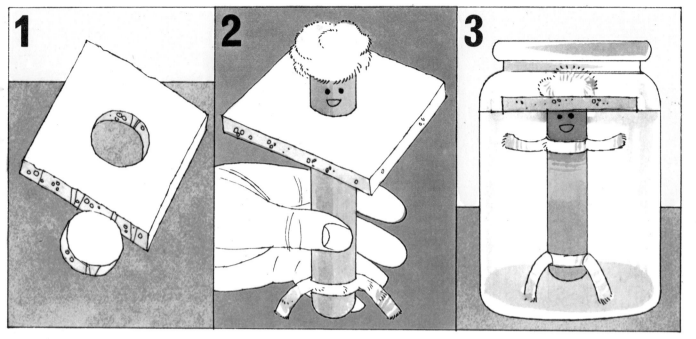

water, but a blue top to the periscope held over the water. This blue top will help to keep the submarine unseen by the enemy ships! You could also make a blue and pink spider from pipe cleaners. See if you can make him all pink and then all blue!

Shipwrecked Sailor and Life-jacket

YOU WILL NEED:
cobalt chloride
polystyrene tile
a knife
a test-tube
a jam jar
pipe cleaners
cotton wool
a wax pencil
a nibbed pen

First make a life-jacket! Cut out a 5-cm. square from the polystyrene tile. Make a round hole in the centre, so that the test-tube just slides in. Its lip will rest on the edge of the hole. **Figure 1.**

Make your sailor. The test-tube will be his body. Use pipe cleaners for his arms and legs. Draw his face on the top of the test-tube with the wax pencil. Fill the test-tube almost to the top with pink cobalt

chloride solution, and plug in a little cotton wool. Use a cotton wool plug for his grey hair. **Figure 2.**

Float your sailor in *warm* water in a jam jar. **Figure 3.**

Watch the colour of the cobalt chloride. Your sailor will go blue in the face! This colour will spread slowly down to his feet.

Put your sailor in a jam jar containing *cold* water. The sailor's feet will go pink and this colour will spread upwards.

Cobalt chloride solution is pink when cold and blue when hot. This is caused partly by loss of water. Heat spreads through liquids mainly by the movement of the tiny particles (molecules) making up the liquid. Scientists say that heat spreads in this way by *convection*. When the cobalt chloride solution was placed in warm water, the heat of the water spread upwards. The cobalt chloride at the top of the tube became warm and turned blue. Soon the heat spread, so that the whole tube became blue. The opposite effect happens when the test-tube is put in cold water.

Use your cobalt chloride solution as invisible ink. Write your secret message with a nibbed pen using pink cobalt chloride solution as ink. Your writing is almost invisible. What do you think you will have to do to make it seen? Warm the paper in front of a fire and your message will appear as blue ink. It will disappear again if the paper becomes moist. To make more invisible inks, turn to page 22.

Pink cobalt chloride solution becomes blue on heating above 50°C. Water changes the blue to pink and the pink writing is almost invisible.

Fun with Potatoes

YOU WILL NEED:
potatoes
sugar
salt
2 short tumblers
a dish
a knife
2 knitting needles
cotton thread
cocktail sticks
a felt pen
a magnifying glass

Look at a potato carefully. What do you see on its surface? Can you see dents? Have a look at them through your magnifying glass. They are what your mother calls the "eyes" of the potato. Count the eyes on the potato. Look at the other potatoes. Do they have eyes too? How many eyes do they have? Take one of the potatoes and into each eye push one end of a cocktail stick. Tie a piece of cotton thread to the end of one of the sticks in the potato. Wind the rest of the thread around the ends of each of the other sticks. The picture above shows you what do do. Does the thread give you a pattern?

The thread is in the form of a spiral. Your potato looks like a prickly monster. To make the pattern

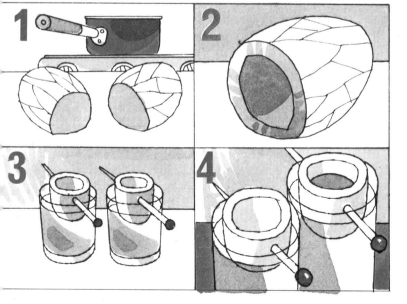

more clear, take a second potato and a felt pen to join the eyes together. This will give you a good spiral.

Have a look at buds on the stems of some plants. Do they form a pattern around the stem? What sort of pattern do they make?

Leave a potato in sunlight for a few days. What do you notice happening to its skin? It slowly turns green.

Your experiments showed that a potato is a stem with its own buds. It is these buds which most people call the eyes of a potato. Buds and twigs on the stems of plants form a spiral pattern. The buds on your potato did too. Your potato turned green in sunlight. Although potatoes grow under the ground, they are not roots. Roots are never green. So potatoes are stems and not roots. They are underground stems which store food.

Potato Puzzle
This experiment will give you ideas for potato-puzzling your friends! Peel two large potatoes. Slice an end off each so they have flat tops. One of the potatoes has to be boiled in water for a few minutes. **Figure 1.**

After the boiled potato has cooled down, hollow out the inside of each potato with your knife. Leave thick walls. You have made two thick potato "cups". **Figure 2**.

Half-fill each tumbler with water. Push a knitting needle through the top of the boiled potato. Hang it inside one tumbler, so that the lower half of the potato is under the water. Do the same for the raw potato. **Figure 3**.

Add half a teaspoonful of sugar to the cup inside each hanging potato. Then leave them for a few hours. What do you see when you come back? One potato is nearly full of liquid. The other is empty! **Figure 4**.

Which one has the liquid in it? This is potato magic that will puzzle your friends! The potatoes *look* the same, but they behave differently.

The water in the tumbler containing the unboiled potato passed through the outside wall of this potato. Water could not pass through the outside wall of the boiled potato in the same way. The boiled potato has no living cells. They were killed by the boiling water. The unboiled potato is a living potato. Its living cells allow water to pass through them.

The passing of water from a weaker solution (in the tumbler) to a stronger solution (inside the cup of the unboiled potato) is called *osmosis*. The cells in the living potato acted as a one-way sieve, allowing water particles (molecules) through them. Scientists call this type of sieve a *semi-permeable membrane*.

Fun with Eggs

YOU WILL NEED:
2 eggs of equal size
dilute hydrochloric acid
2 bowls
salt
an old tablespoon

It's best to do this experiment over the kitchen sink, taking special care. Dilute hydrochloric acid can burn. Be ready to rinse it off with water.

Carefully pour the acid, to a depth of about 1 cm., into a bowl. Place both eggs in the acid. It removes the shells of the eggs. **Figure 1**.

When it has done this, tilt the bowl so that the acid runs away down the sink, but keep the cold tap running. **Figure 2**.

Fill the bowl with fresh water. Using the spoon,

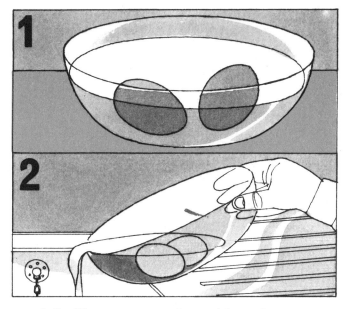

carefully lift one egg and stand it under a strong solution of salt in the other bowl. **Figure 3**.

The egg in the water will swell up. The egg in the salt will shrink. **Figure 4**.

The bowls look the same. Another puzzle for your friends! The size changes take place because of *osmosis*.

Egg in water: The skin of the egg beneath the shell lets tiny water molecules pass through, but not the bigger molecules inside the egg. As well as these bigger molecules (egg-white and protoplasm), there is water in the egg too. But the water enters from the bowl outside faster than the water leaves from inside. Your egg swells, and may burst because it's trying to hold so much water.

Egg in salt: The water moves from the egg into the salt solution faster than outside water enters the egg. The egg loses water and shrinks.

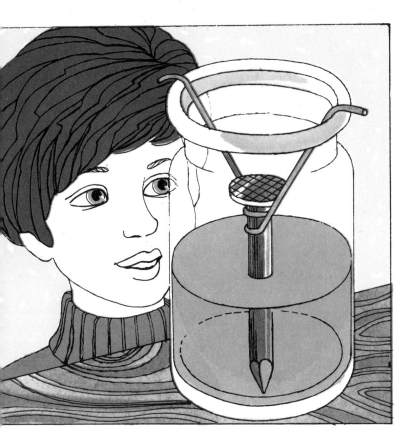

Electric Gas

YOU WILL NEED:
2 carbon electrodes from old dry batteries
2 yoghurt cartons
2 small glass medicine bottles
2 40-cm. lengths of plastic-coated connecting
   wire
a large bowl or dish
a 6-volt battery
2 paperclips
2 clothes pegs
a nail
scissors
a match
vinegar

Have you ever wondered what water is made of? This experiment may provide an answer. It's for the do-it-yourself scientist, because you need to make an electric gasworks! Are you ready?

Let's split water! Make a hole with a nail in the bottom of one of the yoghurt cartons. Push one of the carbon rods through this hole, making a tight fit. Cut a small "arch" in the rim of the carton. In the same way, fix the other carbon rod in the second yoghurt carton. Now wind the bared end of a length of connecting wire to the bottom of one of the carbon rods. Make the join firm by clipping on a clothes peg. Do the same for the other rod.

Fill the bowl almost to the top with water. Lie the medicine bottles under the water, so that they are completely filled. Now place the carbon rods on their carton stands in the water. As you put them in, slip the medicine bottles over the rods, taking care to keep the bottles full. You will need to keep the mouths of the bottles under water. Your bottles now help to keep the rods in place. The two loose ends of the connecting wires should be stripped of plastic coating and connected to the terminals of the battery. Use the paper clips to keep the connections in place. **Figure 1.**

Now watch the carbon rods. Do you see bubbles of gas? Are there bubbles at each of the rods? Add some vinegar to the water in the bowl.

Do the bubbles come faster? The bubbles are gases coming from the water. After your experiment has been running for some hours, you will find each medicine bottle is filling with gas.

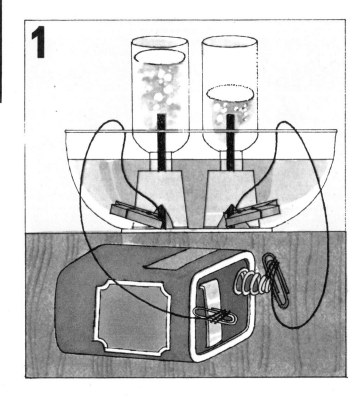

Which bottle has more gas? Trace the connecting wire from the rod beneath this bottle to see whether it is joined to the positive (+) or the negative (−) terminal of the battery. Remove the bottle, taking care to keep your thumb over its mouth so that no gas escapes.

Now to test the gas to see what it is. Turn the bottle upright. Take a lighted match and, after removing your thumb, hold it to the mouth of the bottle. The gas will burn with a loud pop. It is hydrogen. **Figure 2.**

Test the gas in the other bottle in the same way, but this time push a *glowing* match into the gas. The match will relight. The gas is oxygen.

The vinegar added to the water simply helps to make the water a better conductor of electricity. The electricity from your battery splits the water into the two substances which make it. Yes, water is made of two *gases, hydrogen* and *oxygen*! There is twice as much hydrogen (by volume) as oxygen. The hydrogen collects at the negative carbon rod

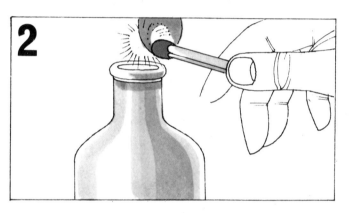

(called the *cathode*). The oxygen gas collects at the positive carbon rod (called the *anode*).

Using electricity in this way is called *electrolysis*. Your experiment is the *electrolysis* of water.

Copper Plating

YOU WILL NEED:
copper sulphate
a 3-volt bicycle lamp battery
two lengths of connecting wire
a jam jar
a teaspoon (one you won't need again!)
a length of bare copper wire
an old tablespoon

Fill a jam jar almost to the top with water. Add two tablespoonsful of copper sulphate and stir until the crystals have dissolved. You can use this solution for copper plating. Iron or steel articles can simply be dipped in to give them a thin layer of copper as a coat. **Figure 3.**

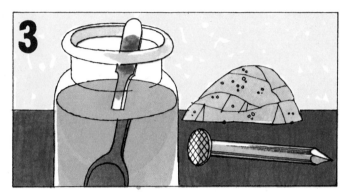

Iron is more active chemically than copper. It replaces copper in copper sulphate solution, making iron sulphate. The replaced copper coats the iron. But copper itself can replace some metals. If it is dipped in silver nitrate solution, beautiful crystals of silver form.

A better method, which gives a longer-lasting coat, is to use an electric current again. For this the article must be clean. To plate an object like a spoon, first clean it thoroughly. Connect it to the negative (−) terminal of the battery, and hang it in the copper sulphate solution. Wind the copper wire around a pencil, to make the wire into a spiral shape.

Connect the copper spiral to the positive (+) terminal of the battery, and hang it in the copper sulphate solution. The spoon and the spiral must not touch in the jar. **Figure 4.**

Copper will soon cover the spoon. The coat looks

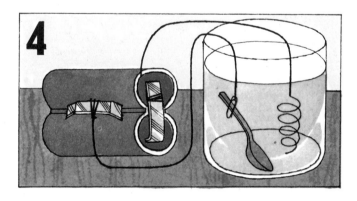

dark in the copper sulphate solution, but when you take the spoon out it will look copper red.

Just as hydrogen is attracted to the negative rod (electrode), so copper is attracted to the negative electrode. The negative electrode (cathode) in this experiment is the spoon.

Invisible Fizz Gas

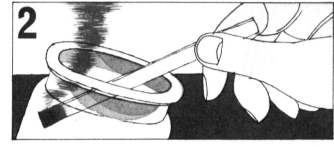

How would you like to make the gas that puts the

fizz in fizzy drinks? Put about four teaspoonsful of fruit salts in a jam jar. Add enough water to cover the fruit salts (about 3-cm. depth of water) and quickly place your cover on the jar. **Figure 1**.

Soon you will have a jar full of invisible fizz gas, a gas which scientists call carbon dioxide. You can't see the gas, so how do you know that your jar is full of it? Light a taper, remove the lid from the jar, and push the lighted end of the taper inside your invisible gas. The flame is put out at once. **Figure 2**.

You can amaze your friends by showing that there is indeed a special gas in the jar: magic carbon

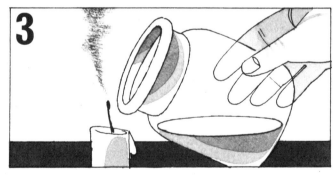

dioxide!

Here is another magical trick with which to surprise your friends. Become a fireman with your own fire extinguisher! Carefully pour your invisible gas over a candle flame. **Figure 3**.

You can guess what will happen. But can your friends? When water is added to fruit salts, carbon dioxide gas is produced. Fruit salts are a mixture of sodium bicarbonate (baking soda) and a solid acid, such as tartaric acid. Acid and baking soda give carbon dioxide. You could make carbon dioxide another easy way by mixing vinegar (an acid) with baking soda, or soda-mint tablets.

Carbon dioxide gas will not allow things to burn in it. This fizz gas will put out flames. Because of this, and because it is also a heavy gas, which is not easily blown away by the wind, it is used in some fire extinguishers.

Your fizz gas turns clear limewater milky. This is how chemists test for carbon dioxide. Make some limewater by dropping a piece of lime (take care—lime can burn) into a bottle of water. Leave for a few hours, shaking occasionally. Limewater will be left at the top as a clear liquid. **Figure 4**.

Pour this clear portion carefully into another bottle. You can label this "Limewater", and use it as a test liquid.

Pour a little limewater on to a clear plastic spoon and hold it in a jar full of fizz gas. **Figure 5**.

The limewater goes milky; the plastic spoon will help you see this change more clearly. Blow some soap bubbles into a jar full of carbon dioxide. See how the bubbles float on top of the invisible gas.

Carbon dioxide is a heavy gas. Because the soap bubbles are *less dense* than carbon dioxide, they will float on the gas in much the same way as wood floats on water.

Use this heaviness of carbon dioxide to amuse your friends. You can pour carbon dioxide from one jar

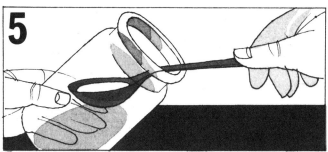

into another containing only air. Both jars will appear empty to your friends. Because carbon dioxide is invisible, no change in the contents of the second jar can be seen.

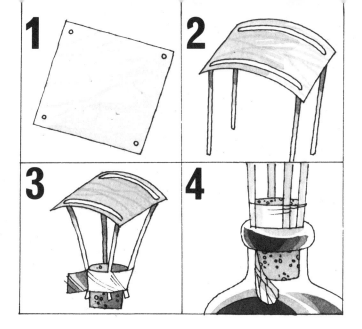

An Ejector Seat

YOU WILL NEED:
strong paper tissue
pipe cleaners
a plastic pill bottle and cork
fruit salts, such as Eno's
water
adhesive tape

To make a parachute for the ejector seat, cut out a square piece of strong tissue paper about 15 cm. × 15 cm. Pierce a hole near each corner. **Figure 1**.

If you wish, you can strengthen these holes by adding ring reinforcement tabs (the ones used on papers holed for ring folders). Take two equal lengths of pipe cleaner, and thread them through the holes in the parachute canopy. **Figure 2**.

Attach the loose ends of the pipe cleaner to the top of the cork ejector seat, using adhesive tape. **Figure 3**.

Now you are ready to fit the explosive charge to your seat! Roll a teaspoonful of fruit salts into a piece of paper tissue and twist the paper until your "charge" is tightly closed. Turn the pill bottle upside-down, add a little water, and then insert the cork tightly, jamming the paper tissue charge inside the bottle. **Figure 4**.

Now turn the seat upright, resting on the cork, and watch the seat eject!

Carbon dioxide gas is formed by the action of water on fruit salts. The pressure produced blows the "seat" from the cork.

The Blue Test Game

YOU WILL NEED:
pencils and paper
small amounts of 12 different foods, such as:
boiled potato
raw potato
bread · biscuit
cooked rice
sugar
a piece of apple
a cooked carrot
an onion
fish fingers
corn flakes
raw meat

You eat to live, but do you know much about what you are eating? Do you know that some foods contain starch? Which foods? This game will help you to find out. It is for two players.

Look at the 12 foods and decide which ones you think contain starch. You are now going to pick your starch team! Toss a coin to decide who has first choice. The winner of the toss picks the food he thinks most likely to contain starch. He writes this down on the top of his list.

Now it is the other person's turn. She makes her choice from the remaining food. This goes at the top of her list. The first person makes his choice for

second on his list, and so on. Soon both of you will have a list of six foods. Set your lists as below.

First Player			Second Player		
	Foods	Points		Foods	Points
A.	. . . . . .	6	A.	. . . . . .	6
B.	. . . . . .	5	B.	. . . . . .	5
C.	. . . . . .	4	C.	. . . . . .	4
D.	. . . . . .	3	D.	. . . . . .	3
E.	. . . . . .	2	E.	. . . . . .	2
F.	. . . . . .	1	F.	. . . . . .	1

You will need the "Points" columns later. First, test the foods for starch.

YOU WILL NEED:
saucers
a medicine dropper
tincture of iodine
starch powder
the 12 foods
a tumbler
a spoon

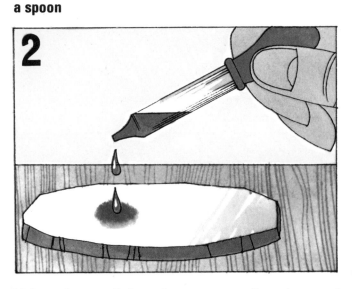

Using the medicine dropper, put five drops of iodine in the bottle. Add water to a depth of about 3 cm. and stir. This is your iodine solution. The next little experiment will show you what to look for when you test for starch. Put some starch powder in a saucer. Add a few drops of iodine solution. **Figure 1.**

What do you see? Where the iodine touches the starch, a blue-black colour appears. Starch goes a blue-black colour in the presence of iodine. This is the test for starch.

Now take turns to test each of the foods to see if they contain starch. Use a clean saucer for each test. It is best to slice the food and soak it with water. Then add a few drops of the iodine solution from the dropper. **Figure 2.**

If you see a blue-black patch, the food contains starch. Take turns with your friend in testing.

How to Score
The food at the top of the list is marked 6 points, the next 5 points, and so on down to the last choice. If the food contains starch, as shown by your test, double the points score alongside the name of the food. If it does not contain starch as shown by your test, then score *no* points. The person whose list gives the most points is the winner of the Blue Test game.

Our food is mainly *fats*, *proteins* and *carbohydrates*. Starch and sugar are carbohydrates. Starch is made up of chains of sugar units joined to form a giant molecule. The saliva in our mouths helps to break down starch into the sugar units for our bodies. Now you know some of the foods which contain starch.

Make a Bean Bomb

YOU WILL NEED:
a small bottle with cork (a small milk bottle will do)
bean seeds
a paper carrier bag

Do you know about the secret power of little plants? Try this experiment. Fill a small bottle with bean seeds. Cover the beans with water and then cork your bottle. Stand the bottle in a paper carrier bag and then completely cover the bottle by folding the bag in half. The beans will be in darkness. Keep the bottle standing upright, with some space above it. Leave your experiment in a safe, warm place for about four days. Then open the bag carefully. What has happened to your cork?

The dry seeds swelled as they took in water. Then as the seeds germinated, developing stems and roots, they grew bigger (expanded) again. These sprouting seeds can push with great force. Your seeds pushed against the sides of the bottle and the bottom of the cork. The cork was able to give way. It popped out. This force of plants is important in nature. For example, over many years, plants can cause even rocks to split.

Sun Seekers

YOU WILL NEED:
2 saucers
cress seeds
blotting paper
scissors

Cut out two circular pieces of blotting paper to cover the inside of the saucers. Place the papers on the bottom of each saucer and wet them thoroughly. Sprinkle the cress seeds over the blotting paper in the saucers. Place one saucer in a dark cupboard. Put the other on a window ledge. The experiment will take several days. Keep both sets

Sowing Seeds

YOU WILL NEED:

seeds, such as mustard, cress, beans, sunflower
wild seeds: sycamore, dandelion
kitchen seeds: apple pips, orange pips, etc.
yoghurt cartons or ice-cream pots
planting medium (bulb fibre, clean sand or
   vermiculite)
a jam jar
a saucer
a polythene bag and an elastic band
a hammer and nail (or spirit burner and paper clip)
adhesive tape
scissors

Try growing different seeds. These can be grown in yoghurt cartons. Make about five holes in the bottom of one of these. You can do it with a hammer and nail, but an easier way is to pierce the plastic carton with a heated wire. A straightened paper clip held in a home-made spirit burner will do fine. (Hold the paper clip with pliers.) Choose the seeds of the plant you want to grow. Soak them

in water for about 24 hours, using the jam jar. **Figure 1**.

Fill the pierced carton about three-quarters full of planting medium. Place your seeds on top of this, and then cover them with more medium (about ½ cm.). Gardeners say that a seed should be covered to twice its own depth.

Label your carton like gardeners label their plants. Stick a cardboard label on the carton with adhesive tape.

Stand the carton in water in a saucer, until the water soaks through to the top. Then let the carton drain. Cover the carton with the polythene bag, using an elastic band to keep it in place. **Figure 2**.

Put the seeds in a warm place. Now try the other seeds. See how they compare for germination and growth. Seeds need water, air and warmth to germinate. The polythene cover prevents the planting medium from drying out.

of seeds well watered. After a few days, see which set of seeds has grown best.

The seeds germinating in the cupboard will show a faster growth of seedlings than the other set.

Take the seedlings from the window ledge, and move them to a spot on the side of the room away from the window. Remember to keep the seedlings watered. Watch the growth of the seedlings closely. What do you notice after several days? They look as if they have been in a gale! **Figure 3**.

The small plants are all bending towards the light. Plants grow faster in the dark. Your plants seek light. These green plants need light for healthy growth.

See if the other seedlings will continue to grow in a dark cupboard. As long as you keep them watered, you may be in for a surprise. Compare these plants, after a few days, with those growing

in the room. What difference do you see? Look at the leaves of the plants and their stems. Measure the length of the tallest "room grown" plant and the tallest "cupboard grown" plant. How do they compare?

Plants grown in the dark tend to be long and thin. The leaf colouring is yellowish. The leaves are small. Green plants need light for healthy growth. Read about the green colouring matter, chlorophyll, and light on page 53.

Colourful Flames

YOU WILL NEED:
a spirit burner
an egg-cup filled with water
a length of wire
a pair of pliers
salt
cream of tartar
boric acid
chloride of lime
copper sulphate
a selection of coins
sugar lumps
a little cigarette ash
lemon juice

This is an exciting experiment for long winter evenings, because you get best results in a darkened room.

When scientists want to find out what is in a substance, they often burn that substance in a flame. The colour of the flame gives them very useful clues. You can be such a scientist today. Make a small loop on the end of a piece of wire. **Figure 1**.

The wire can come from a metal coathanger, or even a large, opened-up paper-clip. Light the spirit burner. Dip the wire loop in the water contained in the egg cup and then burn the loop in the flame.

This will clean the wire. Make sure any paint is burnt off the loop.

Dip the cleaned wire loop into the water and then into some salt. Salt crystals should cling to the wire. Hold the loop in the flame of the spirit burner. **Figure 2**.

The salt will burn. Look at the colour of the flame. It will be a bright yellow. This deep yellow flame tells scientists that *sodium* is present. There is sodium in salt.

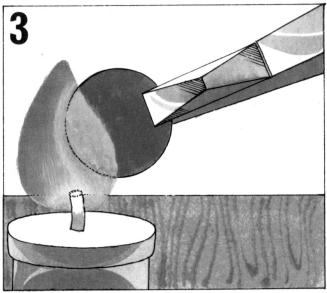

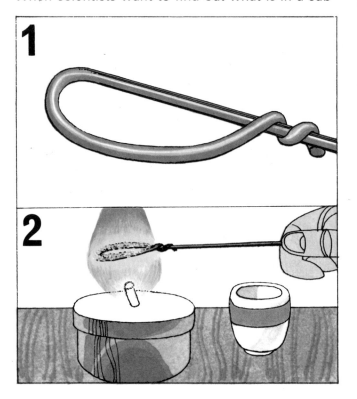

Burn the loop clean and dip it in water again. Test your chemicals in turn by burning them in the flame. Make sure you clean the wire each time. Write down the name of the chemical and the colour flame it gives. Your chemicals are: cream of tartar, boric acid, chloride of lime, copper sulphate and, of course, salt.

Scientists use these flame tests to identify some *elements*. Elements are the "building blocks" which make up chemicals. Here are the colour flames which some elements give:

SODIUM	yellow
POTASSIUM	lilac or violet
BORON	green
CALCIUM	red
COPPER	green-blue

Salt gives a yellow flame. It contains *sodium*. Cream of tartar gives a lilac or violet flame. It contains *potassium*. Chloride of lime gives a red flame. It contains *calcium*. Copper sulphate gives a green-blue flame. It contains *copper*. Boric acid gives a green flame. It contains *boron*.

These colours, which elements show when they are hot, are very important indeed. They enable scientists to find out, for example, what elements are present in the sun, which is 93,000,000 miles away.

Here is a coin game. Put a little salt on the edge of a copper coin. Add two or three drops of lemon juice. Hold the coin with a pair of pliers so that the edge holding the salt and lemon is in the flame. **Figure 3.**

Watch what happens. The flame will turn yellow and then green. This shows that copper is in the coin. Where did the yellow colour come from?

To play the game: See if you can guess which coins contain copper. Ask your friends to do the same. You can try foreign coins too. Test each coin in the flame. Award one point each time the guess is correct. You may have a few surprises!

The flame shows yellow at first because of the sodium in the salt. When the lemon juice has boiled away, the flame goes green. There is copper in the coin.

Do you think a sugar lump will burn in your flame? Let's try. Use your burner, standing it in a saucer for this experiment. Wind the loop of wire around the sugar lump to hold it tightly in place. A pair of pliers will help you here. Hold the sugar lump in the flame. **Figure 4.**

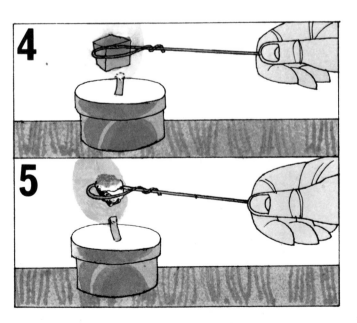

You will not be able to make the sugar burn. It may melt a little and become darkened. That's all.

Try this to make it burn. Take a fresh lump of sugar in the loop. Just touch one corner of the lump with a speck of cigarette ash.

Put this corner in the flame. It will burn with a pale blue flame. Can you see tiny smoke rings too? Hold the burning lump near the flame, so that any drops fall into the saucer. **Figure 5.**

The cigarette ash helps the sugar to burn. While it burns, the sugar changes. The ash does not take part in this change. It is said to be a *catalyst*. This is a substance which changes the speed of a chemical reaction. When the sugar is burnt (oxidised) it breaks down into the elements from which it is made. One of these elements is the black substance carbon. You will be able to see this. The other elements which make up sugar are oxygen and hydrogen.

43

Popping Gas!

YOU WILL NEED:
a jam jar
aluminium baking foil
washing soda
scissors
hot water
a match
detergent
a spoon

Hydrogen is a dangerous gas. This way you can make some safely. Stand the jam jar in the sink and add a few tablespoonsful of washing soda. Cut up some pieces of aluminium foil, about the size of a penny, and add them to the jar. Pour in some hot water—the hotter the better. Stir up the mixture. When it has settled, look at the aluminium foil.

The chemical reaction between the aluminium and the washing soda produces hydrogen. Hydrogen is a gas, and tiny bubbles of it will be seen clinging to the pieces of foil. The bubbles make the foil light enough to float.

Cut a piece of aluminium foil about 10 cm. square and fit it over the jar to form a lid. Press the foil well down over the sides of the jar so that no gas can escape. Make a hole in the foil lid with the match. Now light the match and hold it over the hole.

You will get a small explosion—a squeaky pop. If enough gas collects in the jar, you may find that a steady flame burns at the hole for a short time.

When a mixture of hydrogen and air is ignited, there is an explosion! The squeaky pop that you hear is often used by scientists as a test for hydrogen. The hydrogen burns in the oxygen in the air to form water, although in this experiment not enough water is formed for you to see it. The formula for water is H_2O—that is, two lots of hydrogen to one of oxygen.

Wait two or three minutes before attempting another explosion. This will allow time for more hydrogen to collect around the hole.

Remove the foil lid and add a squirt of washing-up liquid detergent. Stir the mixture or shake it to allow the bubbles to form. Put a lighted match to the bubbles. You have made explosive bubbles of hydrogen.

The hydrogen in the bubbles explodes with a squeaky pop. Hydrogen is the lightest gas in the world. Because of this, it was used in airships to lift them. Most people thought that it was a dangerous gas for the job. You now know why they thought this. Nowadays some scientists believe that hydrogen will be a most important fuel. Liquid hydrogen is used as a fuel in spacecraft.

Making Sherbet

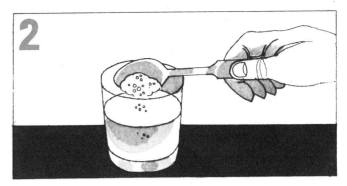

YOU WILL NEED:
citric acid
icing sugar
sodium bicarbonate
a tablespoon
a shallow glass pot with a screw lid
a teaspoon

How about a refreshing drink? Mix together three

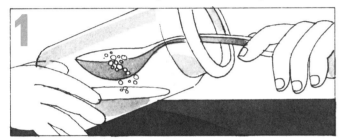

tablespoonsful of citric acid, seven tablespoonsful of icing sugar and one heaped tablespoonful of sodium bicarbonate in the glass pot. Use the back of a teaspoon to grind the mixture into as fine a powder as you can make. **Figure 1.**

This takes time, so be patient. When your powder is ready, screw on the lid to keep it dry. Mix a little of your sherbet with water. **Figure 2.**

What do you see? Try a drink of sherbet. Keep the rest dry for your friends.

When mixed with water, citric acid and sodium bicarbonate make the gas carbon dioxide. (Baking powders are often made of sodium bicarbonate and a solid acid, like citric acid.) Carbon dioxide is the gas which bubbles and gives your drink "fizz".

Caramel

YOU WILL NEED:
sugar
a cup
a frying pan
a wooden spoon

You will need to have your mother's permission for this experiment. It's best also to have the kitchen well ventilated.

Put half a cupful of sugar into the frying pan. Turn on a heating ring of the cooker to a medium heat. The sugar in the pan will melt. Stir slowly with the wooden spoon to prevent the sugar burning. **Figure 3.**

Adjust the heating ring to a low heat, and keep heating the melted sugar until it boils. While you

heat, keep stirring until the liquid becomes dark brown. Then turn off the ring. Move the pan to a cool place on top of the cooker, and leave it to cool. You have made dark brown caramel. It's very hot when first made, so take care. When it is really cool, add some water. Taste your caramel. There may be a surprise in store. **Figure 4.**

Caramel is sugar which has been strongly heated until it is brown. But it is not burnt. The sugar loses water at about 200°C, and slowly changes into brown caramel. Caramel is used as a colouring for vinegar, soups, gravies and other foodstuffs.

Sugar is a chemical compound made of the elements hydrogen, oxygen and carbon. Its formula is $C_6H_{12}O_6$. When sugar is heated, hydrogen and oxygen are removed as water (H_2O). Carbon in the form of sugar charcoal is left behind. This is one of the purest forms of charcoal. Find out all you can about carbon.

Breathing Leaves...

YOU WILL NEED:
fruit salts
a teaspoon
a jug
a jam jar with cover
a yoghurt carton
matches
a spray of fresh leaves

Put about four teaspoonsful of the fruit salts in the jam jar. Place the yoghurt carton, about one-third filled with water, at the bottom of the jar. Put the spray of green leaves standing in the water in the carton. **Figure 1.**

Using the jug, carefully pour water down the inside of the jar so as not to disturb the leaves in the carton. You need enough water to completely cover the fruit salts. **Figure 2.**

Water added to a depth of 2–3 cm. will be sufficient. Quickly place the cover on the jam jar. It will need to be a tight fit. Look inside the jar. You will see bubbling and frothing. A gas is being formed. **Figure 3.**

Soon the gas will stop coming off. Your carton in

the jar will settle down. Take a lighted match and, removing the lid from the jar for a few seconds only, plunge the match into the top of the jar. **Figure 4.**

The match goes out at once. Quickly replace the jam jar cover. Your jar is full of fizz gas—carbon dioxide.

When water is added to fruit salts, carbon dioxide gas is produced. Carbon dioxide will put out flames. That is why your match went out.

Stand your jar in sunlight for about four hours. Now test for carbon dioxide again by putting in a lighted match. The match will stay alight. Where has the carbon dioxide gone?

The leaves standing in sunlight have used up the carbon dioxide. Growing plants take in carbon dioxide from the air and water from the soil. In the presence of sunlight (which is energy from the sun), carbon dioxide, water and the chlorophyll in the plant join together to give food (starch and sugars) for the plant and also oxygen.

This is called *photosynthesis*. Photosynthesis means "to put together by light". Plants produce their oxygen only in the presence of sunlight. Never at night.

Your experiment showed that carbon dioxide was taken up by the spray of leaves. They obtained their water from the partly filled yoghurt carton.

...and Plants

YOU WILL NEED:
a jam jar
a large tin lid
a glass pot (a paste pot will do)
a small plant, with roots
a clothes peg
a plastic bag
string

Half-fill the glass pot with water. Stand the plant

in this, holding it in position with a clothes peg. Put the pot and plant in the middle of the upturned tin lid. Carefully place the jam jar upside down over the plant, and then fill the tin with water. **Figure 1.**

Place the experiment in a dark cupboard for about 12 hours. Then have a look at the level of water in the jam jar. You will find that water from the tin lid has risen inside the jam jar. Why do you think this is?

Your plant used up the oxygen of the air trapped under the jam jar. To make the pressures inside and outside the jam jar equal, water rose up inside the jar to take the place of the oxygen gas that was used up. Plants *breathe*. In sunlight, this *respiration* (breathing), is hidden by the effect of photosynthesis. At night, or in darkness, when photosynthesis cannot take place, plants take in oxygen and give off carbon dioxide. Plant breathing (oxygen used), however, does not cancel out photosynthesis (oxygen made). Photosynthesis is stronger and, on the whole, there is a balance in

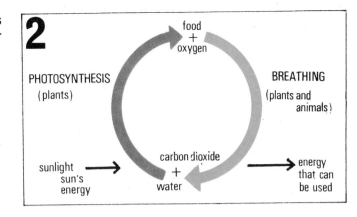

favour of "more oxygen made". Plants and animals breathe. Only in plants does photosynthesis take place. Some scientists say that photosynthesis is the most important chemical reaction in the world. Do you think it is?

This is the cycle in nature. It shows that substances important for the lives of both animals and plants are not used up. **Figure 2.**

Let's see if you can show that water is formed when plants breathe. Find a shrub growing in soil (in the garden, if you have one), and cover a stem with a plastic bag. Tie the ends of the bag so that the twigs and leaves are sealed inside. **Figure 3.**

Leave the bag for several hours. Now have a look inside the bag, but leave it tied. Can you see drops of water? Leave the bag tied on the stem for a few days. Then untie it and find out how much water has been collected. You may be surprised. The water has come from the leaves. This breathing out of water by leaves is called *transpiration*.

Transpiration is important in nature's water cycle. This is the cycle in which water comes down from the clouds in the sky as rain. Then, after filling our needs, it returns to the sky as vapour. The water for the clouds is provided from the surface of the earth by evaporation and transpiration. Evaporation is the changing of liquid into vapour, mainly from the seas and oceans. Transpiration is the second source of water for the clouds.

Candle Magic

YOU WILL NEED:
a household candle
a tin lid to serve as a candle stand
matches
2 microscope slides
an 8-cm. length of glass tubing
a 30-cm. length of bent glass tubing
a clothes peg
limewater
a knife
2 jam jars

Have fun with a candle. Hold a lighted match underneath the candle so that some drops of melted wax fall on to the tin lid. Fix the candle firmly on the lid by standing it on these wax blobs. When the blobs cool, the candle will be secure.

Now light the wick. Look closely at the candle flame. It's a wonderful chemical action. Do you see the different parts (zones) of the flame? How many different coloured parts of the flame can you see? Hold a cold saucer in the top of the flame. You will collect a fine spread of soot. There is *carbon* (soot) in a candle flame. **Figure 1.**

Let's find out some more about the flame. Hold a clean, dry microscope slide just above the wick and keep it there for about 15 seconds. **Figure 2.**

Now take the slide away and have a close look at it. Put it down on a piece of paper and have another look when it has cooled down. Wax collects on the slide. There is some form of wax in a candle flame.

Do the same experiment again. This time hold the slide in the *yellow* part of the flame. Take the slide away. Have a close look at it, first when it is still warm, and then when it has cooled down. Use a clothes peg to hold the 8-cm. length of glass tubing at its middle. Put one end of the tubing in the candle flame *just above* the wick. **Figure 3.**

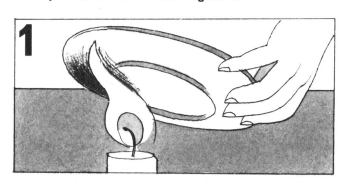

What do you see coming down the tube?

Try to light the gas coming from the tube with a match. With a little patience you can light it. Does the tube's flame look like a candle flame?

Dip the tube into some limewater. Put your finger over the top to trap some limewater in the tube. Hold the trapped liquid above the candle flame for a few seconds. What do you see?

The limewater turns milky. Carbon dioxide gas is formed as the candle flame burns.

Hold a cold knife blade for a moment about 9 cm. above the candle flame. Can you see moisture on the blade?

Water may be formed when a candle flame burns. In fact, further experiments would show that your "moisture" on the blade is water. This is what a candle flame looks like. **Figure 4.**

The paraffin wax is made of hydrocarbons (substances which contain joined-together hydrogen and carbon only). This wax is melted and is drawn up the wick (three strands of plaited string) by *capillarity*.

The melted wax *vaporises* in zone "A". This is a dark inner zone of unburnt paraffin gas.

In zone "B", the paraffin gas splits up into hydrogen and carbon (soot). The carbon is in the form of tiny particles. These, being very hot, glow. They give out light.

The hydrogen and carbon move out from zone "B" and join with oxygen in the surrounding air to give water and carbon dioxide. Scientists call this *oxidation*.

Zone "C" is particularly bright. Here *oxidation* takes place faster than ever, because there is a good supply of oxygen here.

Your experiments showed these different parts of the candle flame. You were able to tap off and then light the "unburnt" paraffin gas. A very famous scientist called Michael Faraday (1791–1867) wrote a whole book about the chemistry of a candle flame.

Now that you know more about a candle flame, try this: Place one end of the bent tubing in the flame, just above the wick. Collect the white gas in a jar. Look at it in the jar. What weird behaviour!

Raise the end of the tube in the flame until it is in the yellow part of the flame. Collect the gas in the same jar. Repeat the collection of gas from the part of the flame just above the wick, but this time use a fresh jam jar.

Cool the contents of the jar under a tap. Look at the bottom. Now add a drop of water. Watch its

behaviour. What do you think is coating the bottom of the jar?

You collected paraffin wax gas from the zone of the flame above the wick. When this gas is cooled (*condensed*), it changes into solid wax. It is a wax coating on the bottom of your jar. The other part of the flame gave you mostly soot from the yellow zone.

Floating Candle

YOU WILL NEED:
a jam jar
a candle
a screw
a screwdriver

Three-quarters fill the jar with water. Fix the screw to the bottom of the candle, using your screwdriver. Now float the candle on the water. Make sure that your screw is not too heavy. The candle should float upright. Light the wick. Leave the candle burning for several hours. What do you notice? You can make a candle with a hollow inside! The water cools the wax at the top of the candle and stops it melting.

Bright Sparks

YOU WILL NEED:
a smooth piece of white card about 25 cm. x 25 cm.
a paint brush
tincture of iodine
hypo (used by photographers)
an egg-cup
a jam jar
an old teaspoon

How would you like to put on a home show for your friends? The first thing you can make is a magic notice for it. Put a little iodine solution in the egg cup. Use your paint brush to completely cover one side of the card with iodine. It will be a brown colour. **Figure 1.**

Add about 2 cm. of water to the jam jar. Now pour

in enough hypo, stirring with the spoon, to make a strong solution. This solution is clear, so that to your friends it will look like water. It is your magic ink. Rinse the paint brush, and then use it to write on the brown piece of card. You can write: "My Home Show". The writing will come up as white letters against a brown background.

Tincture of iodine is a solution of iodine in alcohol. The iodine in your experiment joins with hypo (*sodium thiosulphate*) on the brush to make substances which have no colour. So your writing looks white.

For your home show, here are some "tinklers" with a candle—not bangers, but fun.

YOU WILL NEED:
a candle
a saucer
iron filings
steel wool
salt
rosin
a wooden spoon
thick copper wire
a pair of pliers
a test-tube
a hammer
a piece of cloth

It's best to stand the candle on a saucer, with a sheet of paper underneath. Light the candle and sprinkle a pinch of iron filings over the flame. **Figure 2.**

What do you see? Your iron filings are burning. You can see iron burning in another way. Take a tuft of steel wool. Steel is mostly iron. Spread out the tuft around the top of the handle of the wooden spoon.

Now hold the tuft to the flame. Sparks again! Take the steel out of the flame and watch the tuft burn. **Figure 3.**

A real firework display! Look out for drops falling from the burning steel. What do you think these drops might be?

Large lumps of iron won't burn in your candle flame. But the thin strands, or the tiny filings, will. This is because more of the iron surface is open to the air. The iron joins with the oxygen in the air to form *iron oxide*. You may have seen drops of iron oxide fall from your burning steel wool.

Violinists use rosin to rub on the bow of their instrument. Take a piece of rosin and crush it into a very fine powder. One way is to wrap the rosin in a cloth and grind it with a hammer. **Figure 4.**

The finer the powder you make, the better your experiment will work.

Sprinkle a pinch of the powdered rosin over the candle flame. **Figure 5.**

You have made your own firework! Sparks everywhere, but they are perfectly safe.

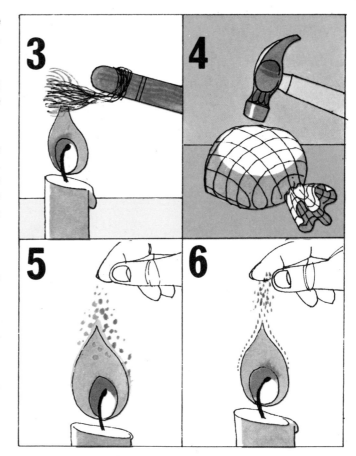

The crushing of the rosin into a fine powder increases the area of the surface which can come into contact with the oxygen in the air. Because of this, each tiny piece of rosin burns very quickly, giving the sparks you saw.

Let's see if you can bring out the best and the worst in a candle flame! First, the best. There may be more to a candle flame than you think. Sprinkle a little salt over the flame and watch the edges of the flame very closely. You will see, just for an instant, an outer zone of the flame appear. **Figure 6.**

It will be coloured yellow. This outer zone is almost invisible, but it is always there. The salt helps you to see it. The salt makes it look yellow. The salt

contains sodium. Sodium burns with a yellow flame.

The worst that can happen to the flame is that it may go out! Here's how to make the flame disappear without blowing and without touching it.

Take a 15-cm. length of thick copper wire and wind it around a test-tube to make the wire into a spiral shape. Hold the spiral with a pair of pliers and gently place it over a candle flame. Make sure that it does not touch the flame—that would be cheating! Soon the candle flame goes out. **Figure 7.**

Copper is a very good conductor of heat. The spiral quickly moves heat from the flame. The flame cools rapidly and goes out.

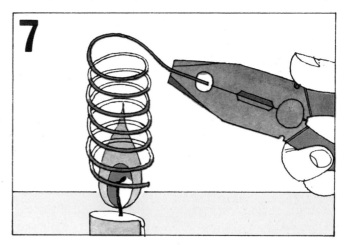

Leaf Secrets

YOU WILL NEED:
whole leaves from different trees, such as:
   sycamore
   copper beech
   oak
   silver birch
   apple
magnifying glass
outer leaves from a cabbage
a brush
a plate
an old washing-up bowl

Have a close look at some whole leaves, using a magnifying glass. See if you can draw the veins in each leaf. This picture will show you what to look for.

You may have seen leaf *skeletons* in the park. They are often damaged. Here is a way to make some perfect ones. They will really show you the veins in a leaf.

Fill your bowl almost to the top with water and put in some outer leaves from a cabbage. Place the bowl out-of-doors in a safe spot. Choose this carefully. The bowl will begin to smell, so make sure that it doesn't annoy your neighbours!

Leave the cabbage leaves to rot in the water. This will take days. When the cabbage is really rotten, add the tree leaves. Again, these must be left for several days until the leaf tissues are soft.

Now take out a leaf and place it flat on a plate. You should be able to gently brush away the soft tissue from the leaf. A beautiful skeleton will be left. Repeat this for all the leaves. **Figure 1.**

Starch Tests

YOU WILL NEED:
a leaf (a freshly cut geranium leaf will do)
a saucer
surgical spirit
boiling water
iodine solution and dropper
a plate

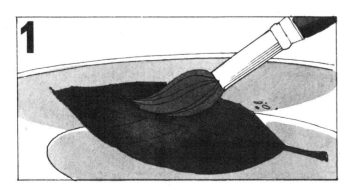

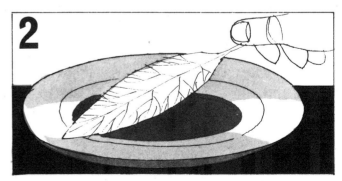

Let's see if leaves contain starch. First the green colouring matter must be taken from the leaf. Using tongs, plunge the leaf into boiling water for about 20 seconds. The boiling water kills the leaf.

Put the dead leaf into the saucer and add enough surgical spirit to cover it. Leave the leaf under the spirit until all the green colour has left the leaf and gone into the spirit. **Figure 2.**

The green colouring matter in plants is called *chlorophyll.* Chlorophyll is very important to plants. It helps to change sap into food for the plant. In your experiment, the surgical spirit (alcohol) dissolved this chlorophyll. The green colour (pigment) left the leaf.

Rinse the leaf in cold water and place it on the plate. Add a few drops of the iodine solution from the dropper. **Figure 3.**

What do you see? Does your leaf contain starch?

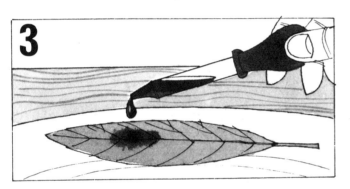

The blue-black stain appears where the iodine touches the leaf. Starch turns a blue-black colour when iodine is added. There must be starch in the leaf.

Leaf Patterns

YOU WILL NEED:
2 green plants
silver foil
paper clips
scissors
a jar

Choose a leaf on one of the plants. Cover it back and front with silver foil. Keep the foil in place with a few paper clips. **Figure 4.**

Now cut out some shapes of foil—strips and small

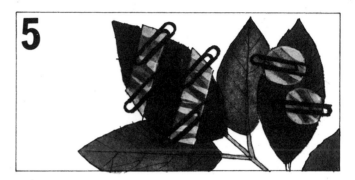

circles will do fine. Put the strips across another leaf, back and front, so that they fit across each other back to back. Again, keep the foil in place with paper clips. **Figure 5.**

Do the same for a leaf on the second plant. Use the circular shapes of foil for this leaf. Now place the plants in sunlight. Water them as usual. Leave them for about three days.

Pluck the silver-foiled leaves from the plants. Remove the foil. Take the chlorophyll from these leaves as described above.

Now place the leaves into iodine solution contained in a jar. **Figure 6.**

What do you see? You will find three magical leaf patterns like those in the picture. One leaf is unchanged by the iodine.

One leaf has stripes and one has circles on blue-black backgrounds, just as in the picture. The completely-covered leaf had no starch in it. It did not change colour in the iodine. The others had starch in them only where the sunlight was able to reach. Starch goes blue-black in the presence of iodine. There was no starch formed under the silver foil. Leaves need both chlorophyll and sunlight in order to make starch. A plant's food is made in its green leaves. Sunlight shining on the leaves gives the plant the energy it needs.

Make a Rock Pool

YOU WILL NEED:
cobalt chloride
a jar
a saucer
a teaspoon
calcium chloride (granular)
a medicine dropper

This is an amazing experiment which will amuse your friends. Take about two teaspoonsful of cobalt chloride and dissolve it, with stirring, in a little water in a jar to make a strong solution. It will be pink.

Draw a little of this solution into the medicine dropper and transfer it to the saucer. Here it will make a small pink pool.

Now for the rocks! Take a lump of calcium chloride, about the size of a pea, and drop it into the middle of your pink pool. **Figure 1.**

Watch closely! The white calcium chloride becomes deep blue, and so does that part of the pool near it. You have a blue rock pool with a pink rim! Soon your rock will disappear. Calcium chloride dissolves in water. But keep watching the colours.

Use the dropper to form a fresh pink pool. This time ask your friends to drop in the calcium chloride. They will be surprised. Try making a bigger pool, with more rocks. It may look like the one above.

Calcium chloride is a well-known chemical used for drying other substances. It has an attraction for water. Because of this, it draws water away from the cobalt chloride. Now cobalt chloride changes colour from pink to blue when it becomes dry. The cobalt chloride near the calcium chloride lost water and changed to a blue colour.

A Green Man

YOU WILL NEED:
cobalt chloride
ammonium chloride
a jam jar
a cup
a teaspoon
scissors
a length of cotton thread
white blotting paper
a spirit burner

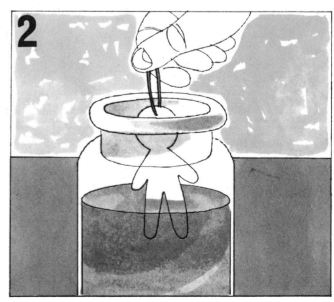

Blue to Red

YOU WILL NEED:
ammonium chloride
use of a gas ring
a test-tube and holder
a pin
a red litmus paper

Place a little ammonium chloride in the test-tube. Add one drop of water before heating. Also hang a damp red litmus paper on a pin in the mouth of the tube. **Figure 3.**

On first heating the ammonium chloride, the litmus paper turns blue—and then red. If you cut down the heat it goes blue again. See how many times you can bring about these two changes. **Figure 4.**

Blue litmus turns red in the presence of an acid. Red litmus turns blue in the presence of an alkali. When ammonium chloride is heated, it splits up into ammonia (an alkali) and hydrogen chloride (an acid). The ammonia turns red litmus blue. The hydrogen chloride turns blue litmus red.

Take three teaspoonsful of white ammonium chloride and stir it with some water in a cup to make a solution. Add this to a solution of cobalt chloride in the jam jar. Mix well. Add water until the jam jar is about half-full. The mixed solution should be pale pink. Cut out blotting paper into the shape of a man, as shown in the picture.

Make a small hole at the top of his head. Thread a length of cotton through this. Now dip your blotter man into the pink solution in the jam jar. You may need to push him in! **Figure 2.**

When he is thoroughly soaked, take him out to dry. Hang him up, with a saucer underneath to catch any drips. The dry man will be almost without colour. Now use your spirit burner to gently warm the man. Hold him by the thread well above the flame. Watch him go bright green! You have made a green man.

Does the colour change back when the man cools down? Try warming the man on a radiator. Does he go green? Now make other shapes that will turn green to amaze your friends.

The blotting paper soaked in the cobalt chloride/ammonium chloride solution is sensitive to heat. Whatever method you use for warming your man, he will go green. Will the experiment work with pipe-cleaners? Try making some pipe-cleaner models. Repeat the experiment with them.

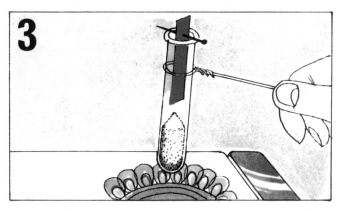

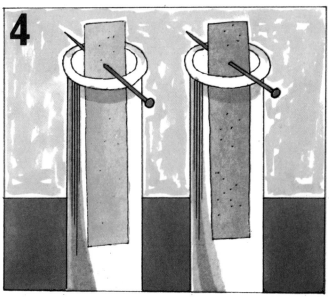

Scientists call this type of cloudy mixture, in which fine particles of one liquid are spread throughout another liquid, an *emulsion*.

Choose an interesting section of your newspaper. Cut out a picture, together with its caption underneath. Try to include some printing in large letters. Place the cutting face upwards on a table and brush your printing fluid over it. Cover it completely. **Figure 1.**

Take a sheet of white typing paper and place it over the wet newspaper cutting. Use a flat block

of wood to press the paper firmly and evenly over the cutting. **Figure 2.**

Take the paper away. What do you see? You have a copy of the newspaper cutting on the typing paper. **Figure 3.**

Your own printing press! Is your print exactly the same as the newspaper cutting? Can you read the writing? Try using a mirror. You can have secret mirror-writing. Form a spy club with your friends!

Your print is a mirror image of the cutting. The left-hand side of your print is the right-hand side of the

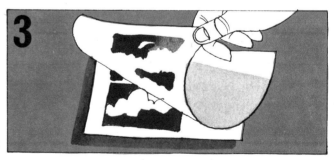

cutting. Just like the image you get in a mirror.

Turpentine is a good solvent. This means that it dissolves certain substances easily. It makes the printing ink on the newspaper cutting wet. Then the wet ink comes off on to your white paper to give a print.

If you *are* going to form a spy club you may need to be able to take fingerprints.

Secret Printing Press

YOU WILL NEED:
a jam jar
turpentine or white spirit
a spoon
a paint brush
a newspaper
a cup
detergent
scissors
a mirror
a block of wood
white typing paper

Make your own secret printing press! Pour half a cupful of turps, or turps substitute, into a jam jar. Add a cupful of water. You will find that the water and turps do not mix. A third substance needs to be added to allow proper mixing. Add some liquid detergent, and stir well. You will get a milky liquid. This will be your "printing fluid".

Making Finger-Prints

YOU WILL NEED:
tincture of iodine
a tin lid
a clothes peg
a spirit burner
white typing paper

Start with a thumb-print. Press down with your thumb on a sheet of white typing paper. **Figure 4.**

Light the spirit burner. Pour a few drops of iodine into a tin lid. Hold the lid with a wooden clothes peg. Now gently warm the iodine in the tin lid. The iodine evaporates. What colour is the iodine vapour?

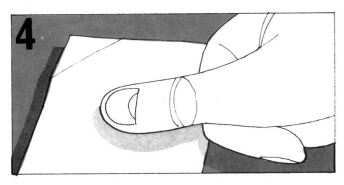

As the vapour appears over the lid, hold the white paper, with the thumb-print on it, above the lid. Your thumb-print will appear as if by magic. **Figure 5.**

Tincture of iodine is a solution of iodine in alcohol. Iodine itself, in ordinary conditions, is a solid element. On heating it changes directly into a purple vapour. Iodine is said to *sublime*. When the iodine vapour cools, it goes back into a solid. You see your thumb-print outlined on the white paper by the solid iodine which has cooled.

Disappearing Ink

YOU WILL NEED:
2 cups
lemon juice
household bleach
an old teaspoon
an egg cup
cotton buds
blotting paper

It's not easy to rub out ink, even with an ink rubber. Here is how to make a liquid ink eradicator. It will remove writing ink from paper.

Pour an egg-cupful of lemon juice into a cup. Add an egg-cupful of water. Stir well. This is your solution 1.

Pour an egg-cupful of household bleach into a second cup. Add three egg-cupfuls of water. Stir well. This is your solution 2.

To remove ink, you first apply solution 1. Dab it on with one end of the cotton bud. After several minutes, blot the solution on the paper. Use the other end of the cotton bud to apply solution 2. What happens to the ink? It will slowly disappear. **Figure 6.**

Blot the paper again. Apply more of solution 1. Blot again. Allow the paper to dry.

The household bleach has a whitening action. The whitening is caused by oxygen from the bleach. This oxygen joins with the colouring matter in the ink to give a new white substance.

Magical Liquid Colour

YOU WILL NEED:
fresh elderberries (dried ones will do)
a paper towel
scissors
a cup and saucer
a yoghurt carton
a glass jar with a screw top
a small nail
a pencil
test-tubes (small glass jars will do)
lemon juice
vinegar · washing soda · a tall bottle

enough, you will see colour changes from red to purple to green.

Elderberry is an *indicator*. This means that it can be used by scientists to test for acids and alkalis. Alkalis are the opposite of acids. Elderberry in a neutral solution (neither acid nor alkaline), like water, is purple. In acid solution it is *red*. In alkaline solution it is *green*. Your experiment shows that vinegar is an acid and that washing soda is an alkali.

Here is an experiment that will entertain your

Some liquids change colour as if by magic. Let's make one of them. Crush the elderberries in a cup. Add a little boiling water and stir well. Filter the elderberry solution when it is cool. The liquid which comes through the filter (the filtrate) is one of your magic liquids. Keep it in a glass jar with a screw top.

Pour a few drops of your elderberry extract from the jar into a test-tube. Add a little vinegar. **Figure 1.**

Do you see a colour change? The magic liquid changes colour from purple to red. Now add some washing soda to the same test-tube. If you add

friends. Take a tall bottle. Fill it almost to the top with water. Now add a little elderberry indicator to colour the water slightly. **Figure 2.**

Put in half a teaspoonful of vinegar. Shake the bottle and then leave the contents to settle. Add three or four pieces of washing soda. **Figure 3.**

Watch them drop to the bottom. There they will dissolve. Look at the different colours in the bottle. If the bottle is not disturbed you will get different-coloured layers. **Figure 4.**

The vinegar (acid) colours your indicator red. The

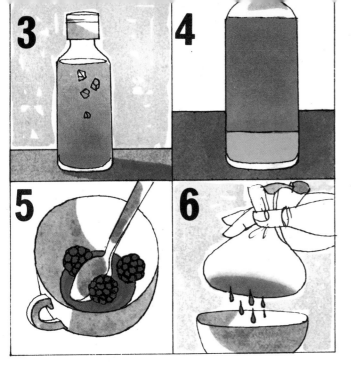

phenolphthalein on its label of ingredients. Make sure you ask your mother first.

Pour a little surgical spirit into the saucer. Add the pill and crush it in the spirit, using the spoon. Mix together well. This liquid is your indicator. Test its colour changes in an acid and in an alkali.

Phenolphthalein solution is pink in alkaline solution and colourless in acid or neutral solution.

Some Tricks
Dilute your phenolphthalein solution with water. Rub your friend's cheek with this weak solution. Dip your own hand in washing soda solution. Press it on your friend's cheek to produce a red hand-print! You can give yourself a clown's nose and pink ears too!

washing soda (alkaline) gives a green colour at the bottom. But this green colour will slowly spread upwards. Scientists say that the molecules of liquid which started at the bottom are spreading by *diffusion*.

You can make indicators from red cabbage, red rose petals, beetroot and blackberries. **Figure 5.**

Treat each of them as you did the elderberries. If you don't want to filter, simply strain the extract through a cloth each time. **Figure 6.**

Find out what colour changes these indicators undergo when they are added to acid and alkaline solutions. Having made your indicators, it is interesting to test well-known substances to see whether they are acid, or alkaline, or just neutral. You could try salt water, fresh milk, sour milk, boric acid, saliva from your mouth, soapsuds, dilute ammonia solution, bicarbonate of soda, lemon juice, orange juice, starch in water, honey in water and bleaching powder—to name but a few! Make a list and write down what happens when you add each indicator (or just your elderberry indicator) to them.

An Indicator

YOU WILL NEED:
surgical spirit
a teaspoon
a saucer
a laxative pill

This is how to make a famous indicator with a long name. It is called *phenolphthalein*. You are going to get it from a laxative pill. Use any pill which has

All Change!

YOU WILL NEED:
phenolphthalein
vinegar
dilute ammonia solution
a medicine dropper
three tumblers

Line up your tumblers in a row. Put three drops of phenolphthalein in the first glass, three drops of ammonia in the second glass and 15 drops of vinegar in the third glass. To your friends, the glasses look empty. Add water to the first glass. It shows clear. Pour the contents of this glass into the second. It goes pink. **Figure 7.**

Then pour this pink solution into the last glass. It goes clear again. **Figure 8.**

You know the explanation, but your friends will be baffled.

When the contents of the second glass are mixed with the third, the overall solution must be acidic. That is why you use more vinegar than ammonia.

Water from Air

YOU WILL NEED:
a tin with a press-top lid
ice
salt
a tablespoon
a narrow block of wood, 10 to 15 cm. long
a brick
a wooden box
a saucer
a pan

This experiment may surprise you. First make some crushed ice. A good way to crush ice is to place it in a corner of a box. Then bang the ice with a brick.

Mix about eight tablespoonsful of the crushed ice with two tablespoonsful of salt in a pan. Make sure the outside of the tin you are going to use is quite dry. Now spoon your mixture of ice and salt into the tin. Press down the lid. Stand your tin on the narrow wooden block. Watch the outside of the can closely. After about 20 minutes you will see frost forming on the can. Scrape some off into a saucer and have a close look. **Figure 1.**

Where do you think the frost came from? Air is a mixture of gases. It contains nitrogen, oxygen, argon, carbon dioxide and *water vapour*. This water vapour in the air is essential to life. Without this moisture that we breathe, we could not live.

When the air near the can is cooled it becomes over-full of water vapour. Your "freezing mixture" in the can cooled the air near it. Some of the water vapour changed (*condensed*) to liquid water. This liquid water froze on the very cold surface of the can. It made a white coating of *hoar-frost* on the outside of the can. The block of wood under the can helped to keep the can cool by *insulating* it.

Measuring Water Levels

YOU WILL NEED:
2 medicine bottles of the same size
a small plant with roots
Plasticine
squared paper
several elastic bands
a pencil

Clean the roots of the plant under a slow-running tap. Fill the medicine bottles with water. Carefully thread the roots of your plant through the narrow neck of one of the bottles, so that the plant is upright. A pencil will help you to guide the roots into position inside the bottle.

Seal the neck of this bottle with Plasticine. The stem of the plant should not touch the neck of the bottle. Seal the second bottle with Plasticine. **Figure 2.**

Cut two strips of squared paper, and attach them with elastic bands to the flat sides of the bottles. Using the pencil, mark the level of water in each bottle on the squared paper. Place the bottles on a window ledge. Leave them for some days. Come back now and again to check the water levels. Each time, mark the water level for each bottle.

Do the levels in each bottle change? Can you explain what you see? Measure how much the water levels change.

The water level in the bottle containing the plant goes down. This is because the roots of the plant are taking the water. The water level in the other bottle will stay the same.

Water into Vapour

YOU WILL NEED:
a spirit burner
a home-made tripod stand as on page 12
an old metal plate
a tin lid
sand
a knife
an onion
a wooden clothes peg

First use your old tin plate as a cook's chopping board. Cut the onion in half. Then slice this half into smaller pieces. Chop the onion finely.

Put the onion pieces into the tin lid. Cover the old tin plate with sand. Now put the tin lid, standing on the sand, in the middle of the plate.

Use your tripod stand to support the plate over the spirit burner. **Figure 3.**

Now light the burner under the tripod. Watch! What do you see? Turn over the onion pieces now and again with your knife. Don't let them burn. When the onion looks dried out, put out the spirit burner. Remove the hot tin lid, using a wooden clothes peg to hold it. Stand the hot lid in a safe place to cool. Have a close look at the onion pieces. How have they changed? The water contained in the onion was driven off by the heat from your spirit burner. You saw water vapour coming up from the onion in the tin. The liquid water was changed into a vapour. It joined the water vapour already in the air. The onion pieces at the end looked different because they had lost their water. They are said to be *dehydrated*.

Try the same experiment with pieces of lettuce.

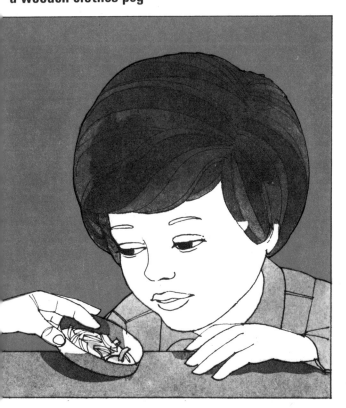